Natural Saints

Natural Saints

*How People of Faith Are Working
to Save God's Earth*

Mallory McDuff

OXFORD
UNIVERSITY PRESS

2010

OXFORD
UNIVERSITY PRESS

Oxford University Press, Inc., publishes works that further
Oxford University's objective of excellence
in research, scholarship, and education.

Oxford   New York
Auckland   Cape Town   Dar es Salaam   Hong Kong   Karachi
Kuala Lumpur   Madrid   Melbourne   Mexico City   Nairobi
New Delhi   Shanghai   Taipei   Toronto

With offices in
Argentina   Austria   Brazil   Chile   Czech Republic   France   Greece
Guatemala   Hungary   Italy   Japan   Poland   Portugal   Singapore
South Korea   Switzerland   Thailand   Turkey   Ukraine   Vietnam

Copyright © 2010 by Oxford University Press, Inc.

Published by Oxford University Press, Inc.
198 Madison Avenue, New York, New York 10016

www.oup.com

Oxford is a registered trademark of Oxford University Press

Library of Congress Cataloging-in-Publication Data
McDuff, Mallory D.
Natural saints : how people of faith are working to save God's earth / Mallory McDuff.
p. cm.
Includes bibliographical references (p.) and index.
ISBN 978-0-19-537957-0
1. Human ecology—Religious aspects—Christianity. 2. Environmental degradation—Religious
aspects—Christianity. 3. Conservation of natural resources.
4. Environmental protection. 5. Christian stewardship. I. Title.
GF80.M375   2010
333.72—dc22   2009048418

3 5 7 9 8 6 4 2

Printed in the United States of America
on acid-free paper

To Ann and Larry McDuff

Acknowledgments

I am grateful to the many people of faith in churches and religious environmental organizations who shared their stories and allowed me to bear witness to their work. For reviews of various chapters, I thank Lyn O'Hare, Harry Shallcross, and members of the faculty writing group at Warren Wilson College, including Catherine Reid, Carol Howard, David Abernathy, John Brock, Ben Feinburg, and Michael Matin. Sarah Urquhart introduced me to the concept of natural saints as featured in her artwork. Funding from Warren Wilson College and GreenFaith supported this research.

Many individuals interviewed for the book also took the time to review chapters, and I thank LeeAnne Beres, Cassandra Carmichael, the Reverend Brian Cole, Vicki Garlock, Brigitte Gynther, the Reverend Fletcher Harper, Stan Hubbard, Tronn Moller, Sister Suzanne Moynihan, Brownie Newman, Jill Rios, Bob Rodriguez, and Will Harlan.

Warren Wilson College students in the 2009 Methods and Materials in Environmental Education class read drafts of chapters and provided constructive feedback. Thanks to Sadie Adams, Johanna Anderson, Lauren Bangasser, Vanessa Emery, Ethan Frei, Sea Gisondo, Jordan Gregson, Tyler Lavenberg, Rose Powell, Ansley Rawlins, Abigail Trajtenberg, Sarah Wishnick, and Brett Wyatt.

I express my profound gratitude to Andy Reed for his copyediting skills and to Cynthia Read, the religion editor, and Jennifer Kowing, the production editor, at Oxford University Press.

Lastly, I thank my daughters, Maya and Annie Sky, who attended church services across the country with me during the research for this book.

Contents

CONTENTS

Natural Saints

Introduction

The Doxology and a Communion of Saints

Praise God from whom all blessings flow
Praise him all creatures here below
Praise him above ye heavenly hosts
Praise Father, Son, and Holy Ghost. Amen.

My family always sang the doxology as a blessing at sacred gatherings. My grandfather, an Episcopal priest, would ask everyone to gather hands in a circle around the Thanksgiving supper table. "Larry," he would say to my father in his deep southern drawl, unique to the Mississippi Delta, "would you lead us in singing the doxology?" With my grandfather's accent, two-syllable words became three, and a simple request became an invocation. In response, my father would sing the word "Praise" in his gentle baritone that led our church choir, and we children would follow with the words we knew by heart. We sang the doxology in dining rooms and hospital rooms, through sunny weather and downpours, amid giggles of children at play and tears at the death of our parents.

As an adult, I feel the accumulated power of the words from the hymns, the Book of Common Prayer, and Bible verses repeated week after week, year after year, in Episcopal churches throughout the South. All those years, my prayers were praising God and *all* creatures here below, but this connection between my faith and my environmental work was not obvious to me until I was in my forties. While my parents preached conservation through their actions, the words of my faith mirrored our family's then radical acts in the small town of Fairhope, Alabama, where we gave up trash services or driving for

Lent. No other families in our town called the waste management company on Mardi Gras to cancel their trash pickup for forty days (and this was before recycling).

Did my parents consider the conservation ethic inherent in both their Lenten discipline and the liturgy, such as the Prayers of the People? "For the good earth which God has given us and for the wisdom and will to conserve it, let us pray to the Lord." I think they did, but for them, the connection wasn't intellectual or abstract. In her book *Leaving Church*, Barbara Brown Taylor writes, "Living in relationship with creation is saving my life now."[1] To my parents, the relationships among God, their faith, and the earth became their life.

Faith, not politics, informed their Christian conservation ethic. We never said the words "environment" or "conservation." But to conserve energy, we tried not to use the air conditioner in the summer or central heat in the winter. My parents, who died before their time, lived in a communion of natural saints, creating spiritual community through Christian stewardship of the earth.

This book aims to document the life of the church that my children will see as relevant to both their spiritual *and* ecological communities. The research reveals the stories of Christians using their faith as a moral mandate for saving the environment. The journey allowed me to reclaim my own Christian identity, as a southerner living in the progressive community of Asheville, North Carolina, where the word "Christian" sometimes evokes images of televangelists. Before beginning this book, I faced a room of thirty people gathered for a workshop on greening congregations. "The church is where we go to be our best selves," said one participant. "If we're trying to be better stewards of the earth, isn't church the place to start?"

The primary purpose of this book is to gather concrete stories and strategies to answer this workshop participant on a larger scale. My research addresses one key question: How do people of faith integrate the environment into their ministries? The stories introduce contemporary church leaders and parishioners who are working to define a new environmental movement, where justice as a priority for the church includes a clean and safe environment for all. Through their works, these Christians have redefined traditional ministries through the lens of the environment, creating more relevant and meaningful churches.

The Growth of Faithful Environmentalists

From access to local foods to suburban sprawl, environmental issues impact our health, our children, our pocketbooks, and our spiritual communities. The increasing rate of environmental degradation and decreasing connection to the outdoors ultimately reflect a crisis of the spirit. Studies have shown that a lack of connection to the natural world affects children's emotional, cognitive, and spiritual development, as documented in Richard Louv's *Last Child in the Woods*. In Louv's book, a young person asks if God and Mother Nature are married.[2] The church has the potential to tap into this spiritual connection between the environment and human communities to transform our modern relationship with the earth and our faith.

Throughout history, religion has played a key role in societal shifts, from the abolition of slavery to the civil rights movement. "No other group of institutions can wield the particular moral authority of the religious," writes Mary Evelyn Tucker in *Worldly Wonder: Religions Enter Their Ecological Phase*.[3] Across the United States and indeed the world, diverse faith communities are responding to environmental degradation with both reflection and action. All faith traditions, from Judaism to Buddhism, have a theological mandate to protect the earth. This book, however, highlights the Christian faith, due to the significant percentage of the United States population that identifies as Christians and the diversity of churches—evangelicals to mainline Protestants—that have come together around the environment.

A 2004 study by the Pew Forum on Religion and Public Life showed strong consensus for environmental protection across religions, in contrast to issues such as abortion and gay marriage, which divide and politicize religions.[4] According to this study, 78 percent of Americans identify as Christians, making them a powerful force in the electorate.

The Sierra Club's publication *Faith in Action* reveals that 67 percent of Americans say that they care about the environment around them because it is God's creation.[5] This report presents the initiatives of one faith community in each of the fifty states, including water conservation at St. Mark's Presbyterian Church in Tucson, Arizona, and opposition to new coal-fired power plants by the Texas Christian Life Commission.

The examples above address the plea of renowned scientist E. O. Wilson, who has called for the involvement of churches in the environmental crisis. Raised Southern Baptist in Mobile, Alabama, Wilson frames his book *Creation* as a letter to a pastor: "I write to you for your counsel and help."[6] He asks for help "because religion and science are the two most powerful forces in the world today, including especially [in] the United States. If religion and science could be united on the common ground of biological conservation, the problem would soon be solved." There is a strong biblical basis for environmental stewardship, beginning with the formation of Adam in Genesis 2:7 from the "dust of the ground." The psalms are poems to creation, with all creatures bearing witness to God. Indeed, the story of Noah's ark involves a covenant that God made with Noah and all creatures.

The history of the American religious environmental movement reveals significant milestones, such as a 1987 report by the United Church of Christ that documented environmental injustices related to the location of toxic waste facilities based on race and socioeconomic class. Following the publication of this report, the National Religious Partnership for the Environment was created in the 1990s, followed by Interfaith Power & Light in 2000. The National Council of Churches Eco-Justice Program became another leader in religious environmentalism. Cassandra Carmichael, the director of the Eco-Justice Program, said that churches disagree about a lot of topics, but they can typically agree on three things: the need to work for peace, the need to eradicate poverty, and the need to care for God's creation. These three charges are central to stewardship of the earth and the potential for God's people to affect positive change to that end.

Most major denominations have issued environmental statements such as the Evangelical Climate Initiative statement signed in 2006 by eighty-six evangelical leaders. HarperOne published *The*

Green Bible, with commentary by leading religious environmentalists.[7] The religious environmental group Earth Ministry partnered with Ken Burns and his PBS film *The National Parks: America's Best Idea* to distribute a religious study guide and DVD of clips from the film to churches across the country. The organization GreenFaith has helped churches in New Jersey to install solar panels, bearing public witness to energy stewardship. Rabbi Larry Troster, director of the GreenFaith fellowship program told me, "We are in the big bang of the religious environmental movement. There is true momentum."

The use of religious rituals, greening infrastructure, and worship services are some of the ways that churches are tapping into their moral authority to protect God's earth. Books such as *A Greener Faith: Religious Environmentalism and Our Planet's Future* document the history, growth, and potential of this movement worldwide.[8] As one example, the documentary *An Inconvenient Truth* was shown in more than a half million faith communities around the country. Getting this film into churches helped to underscore the moral urgency of climate change and provided a public example of the power of churches to educate their parishioners on environmental issues. The word *stewardship* means "responsible, caring power." Churches have the potential to integrate their stewardship of the earth with prayer for our planet and in doing so evoke a spiritual transformation. As God speaks in Numbers 35:33–34: "You shall not pollute the land in which you live.... You shall not defile the land in which you live, in which I also dwell" (NRSV).

Finding Natural Saints: People and Places of Conviction

To help identify sites for my field visits, clergy and lay leaders provided names of churches and organizations engaged in faith-based activism for the environment. Through my participation in the GreenFaith fellowship program, I had the unique opportunity to interact with religious environmental leaders across the country, many of whom are featured in this book. My goal was to find sites that reflected a range of strategies in religious environmentalism and a diversity of environmental issues, denominations, and racial, ethnic, and socioeconomic backgrounds of parishioners. Many of the chapters include an important interfaith dimension, but the fieldwork focused on churches and Christians, in order to limit the scope of the research.

During these field visits, I made observations, conducted interviews, and led focus groups to document the responses of churches to pressing environmental issues like climate change. My research used the technique of participant observation to gather data: I attended church services, participated in staff meetings, and shadowed staff and community members. The fieldwork enabled me to experience these church institutions as a mother with two children, an academic, and an environmentalist. A collection of small grants covered my travel expenses throughout 2008 and 2009 when I conducted research and taught at Warren Wilson College, a Presbyterian college with a strong environmental mission. The field visits, lasting three to five days, were the foundation of the research and allowed me to be a witness to environmental action "on the ground." Interviews conducted during these field visits were the source for the direct quotations in the book.

The stories collected are a testimony to people doing important work that dates back to the early church, the work of saints living in community. One study of churches engaged in environmental work found that a core group of committed people instigated the efforts in most congregations.[9] These initiatives did not require rewriting of the entire church mission; rather, the efforts needed people of faith who cared about place and each other.

As one example, All People's Church in inner-city Milwaukee transformed its feeding ministry through a small garden that employs youth during the summer, providing job skills as well as produce. At the end of services during the summer, the gardening director distributes fresh produce from the back of the sanctuary. Churches provide a foundation of traditional ministries—including providing food and responding to natural disasters—that become more relevant when viewed in the context of our natural environments. More important perhaps, faith communities offer a perspective of hope, which is much needed in the environmental movement.

In his book *Making Saints*, Kenneth Woodward defines a saint as "someone through whom we catch a glimpse of what God is like—and of what we are called to be."[10] My research sought out people and institutions that met that definition. The chapters that follow introduce natural saints, people living God's love in stewardship of the earth. These saints include a former marine biologist working in a faith-based organization, an environmental educator, an organic gardener turned priest, a lawyer, and a pastor. Each chapter highlights real people engaged in one of the following ministries: protecting human dignity, feeding the hungry, creating sacred spaces, responding to natural disaster and rebuilding, promoting justice, making a pilgrimage, educating youth, and bearing witness.

In each chapter, the book examines the importance of that ministry to the church and highlights that work in diverse places, such as the agricultural fields of southern Florida and the mountains of North Carolina. Each chapter then introduces people of faith who are living out their convictions in God and the environment around them. We enter their spiritual communities to see how an environmental context can transform traditional church ministries. Lastly, the chapter highlights key lessons learned and concludes with a personal reflection revealing the impact of these encounters on my own faith and environmental ethic.

To remain relevant, we in the church must look beyond our parish walls to the environment around us and ultimately within us. Isaiah 55:12 says: "For you shall go out in joy, and be led back in peace; the mountains and the hills before you will burst forth into song, and all the trees of the field will clap their hands" (NRSV). This journey revealed many different versions of a compelling story—the story of churches weaving love of the Lord into care for the environment. This research allowed me to bear witness to one of my grandmother's favorite hymns:

I sing a song of the saints of God, patient and brave and true.
Who toiled and fought and lived and died for the Lord they loved
    and knew.

And one was a doctor and one was a queen, and one was a
    shepherdess on the green. They were all of them saints of
    God and I mean, God helping, to be one too.

If I could encounter these rich stories in my small journey, these natural saints are among us all. Ultimately, this work must happen in
our home parishes, our own churches.

After a summer of visiting churches, my then two-year-old
became adept at pointing out churches as we drove. "That's a red
church," she would say. "That's a brown church." At the end of the
summer, she exclaimed, "I want to go to *our* church!" Indeed, our
stewardship of God's good earth starts at home with the natural
saints among us.

Protecting Human Dignity

Fair Food, Farmworker Rights, and the Church

How does God's love abide in anyone who has the world's goods and sees a brother or sister in need and yet refuses to help?

— 1 John 3:17 (NRSV)

This agreement [CIW-McDonald's] represents a tremendous step forward in the struggle for dignity and justice for farmworkers and the transformation of the agricultural industry toward greater respect for human rights.... Subway and Chipotle and all the rest of the fast food companies ... continue to offer explanations, rationales, and excuses for business practices and policies that do not meet the standard of a basic tenet of Christianity—treat your neighbor as yourself.

—Rev. Michael Livingston, president,
National Council of Churches[1]

The fields around Immokalee, Florida, produce one-third of all the tomatoes eaten by consumers in the United States. This level of production has relied on enslaved labor, recently brought to the nation's attention through a coalition of immigrant farmworkers. One case of slavery involved more than a dozen workers who were beaten, locked in a U-Haul truck, chained, and forced to go to the bathroom in a corner of the truck.[2] This chapter describes a unique partnership between churches and the Coalition of Immokalee Workers, a farm-worker organization, in its Campaign for Fair Food, which strives for fair wages, a code of conduct, an end to slavery in the fields, and a voice for farmworkers (fig. 1.1).

This struggle for human dignity included a ten-day fast by farm-workers in 2003 in front of the Taco Bell headquarters in Irvine, California, one of many tactics used during a four-year campaign that ultimately pressured Taco Bell to agree to a wage increase and a code of conduct for workers. After nine days of fasting, several workers had been hospitalized and many were sick, due to cold rains that continued throughout the fast. In the midst of sacrifice, the celebratory spirit of the campaign prevailed, with a local high-school band playing folk music, farmworkers dancing with priests, and students talking with union leaders. As the tenth day of the fast approached, the Reverend Noelle Damico, the national coordinator of the Fair Food Campaign of the Presbyterian Church (USA), called on religious leaders across

Figure 1.1 Throughout its history, the Coalition of Immokalee Workers has involved people of faith as strong allies in the fight for human dignity. Photo by the author.

the country to write letters asking the farmworkers to end their fast, with a commitment that the religious community would take up their campaign in force during the Lenten season and beyond.

The declining health of the workers led to their decision to end the fast on the tenth day with an Ash Wednesday service, breaking the fast with holy bread and drink. "Then I broke this bread of justice, love, and hope and passed it among the fasters. . . . All I can say is that I palpably felt the presence of the living God and I will never forget it," Rev. Damico wrote in a journal documenting her experience in supporting the workers.[3]

After the service, a small group of farmworkers, children, and religious leaders walked to the locked doors of the Taco Bell headquarters, said a prayer for healing, knelt, and slid letters from national religious organizations under the door, along with thousands of postcards from farmworkers in Immokalee. In her journal, Rev. Damico wrote of the power that people of faith have as consumers, as a moral voice to seek change consistent with God's intention for our world. "Nobody thought that 3,500 farmworkers could take on the largest fast-food industry in the U.S.," she said. "I now truly have faith in things that are yet [un]seen." For as long as there have been Goliaths, there have been Davids as well.

Basic human rights, such as the right to freedom of expression, the right to life, liberty, and security, and the right to freedom from torture, remain the building blocks of human dignity.[4] If humans are created in the image of God, then people of faith have a responsibility to work for justice for all people, especially the marginalized or those who lack a strong voice due to systemic oppression. The work of Christians protecting human dignity has strong ties to the end of World War II and the realization that organized religion would need to be a part of the creation of a new world. Ecumenical organizations were established, such as the World Council of Churches, which was created in 1948 and issued a declaration highlighting the significance of human rights to the work of the church. Certainly, religious institutions have been complicit in human rights abuses throughout history, but there is a strong theological mandate for the protection of human rights both around the world and in local communities.[5]

The story of churches and farmworkers promoting human dignity in Immokalee is one that digs deep to the roots of sustainable food. The Coalition of Immokalee Workers has used creative organizing tactics—theater, boycotts, songs, and prayer—to leverage agreements with some of the leading giants of the fast-food industry for a one-cent increase per pound of tomatoes, the only real increase in wages since 1978.[6] This wage increase almost doubled the rate paid per thirty-two-pound bucket picked. The story of how this group of immigrants took on Taco Bell, McDonald's, Subway, Burger King, Chipotle, and Whole Foods Market reflects how churches have taken on a biblical mandate to protect human dignity as an essential part of sustainable food systems. Diverse denominations have supported this struggle for human rights, beginning with the United Church of Christ, which first endorsed the Taco Bell boycott in 2001 and remains a strong religious ally of the farmworkers today.

This chapter tells the stories of Romeo Ramirez, an immigrant who went undercover to aid the slavery investigations, and Tom O'Brien, a white retiree and amputee in a wheelchair who organized boycotts of Burger King with parishioners from St. Columbkille Catholic Church. The lessons learned include having faith in the improbable, integrating religious rituals into the tactics of grassroots groups, viewing the church as a partner for justice, realizing the power of the church as a place for reconciliation, and recognizing human dignity as a component of sustainable food systems.

Faith in the Improbable

Thirty miles had never been so far away. The drive from Naples, Florida, east to Immokalee mimicked the experience of leaving a metropolitan city and landing in a Latin American agricultural village. The initial three miles of Immokalee Road from Naples featured gated communities with names like Pebblebrook Lake and Heritage Bay. The landscape of sprawl in Naples included the ubiquitous corporate icons of Holiday Inn Express, Shell stations, Target, and Starbucks.

A few miles outside Naples, however, the landscape shifted to a scrub-pine ecosystem with mobile homes rather than elegant town-houses as the primary places of residence. Expansive agricultural fields with orange trees or tomato plants took the place of palm trees, and small signs identified the owners of the fields. Under the hot sun, workers picked produce; the fields were dotted by large dump trucks to transport fruits and vegetables, dilapidated school buses to transport workers, and blue portable toilets to hold human waste.

The drive led me to the town of Immokalee (which, some people note, "rhymes with broccoli"), home to farmworkers who gathered in a parking lot at four o'clock each morning in hope of a day's work from individual growers.[7] The main street of downtown housed a Family Dollar, Mimi's Piñatas, small Mexican restaurants, and Friendship House Shelter. People used bikes as their primary form of transportation. Mobile homes lined the side streets; as many as fifteen people lived in one trailer. Often, four people shared a twelve-by-twelve-foot room with mattresses on the floor. The rent for a run-down trailer located close to the parking lot where workers gathered in the early dawn could go as high as $1,500 a month.

With its bright orange stucco walls, the community center of the Coalition of Immokalee Workers (CIW) was located adjacent to this parking lot. On the benches outside the community center, farmworkers spoke a variety of languages, including Spanish and Haitian Creole, lending Immokalee an atmosphere that integrated cosmopolitan with rural agricultural. In 2009, these workers earned an average of $9,000 a year, pieced together from daily wages based on the pounds of tomatoes picked for individual growers. Some of this money was sent to families in their home countries.

At work in the community center that day was Gerardo Reyes-Chavez, a tall, angular man with deep brown eyes and an engaging smile. Many of the media photos documenting the Campaign for Fair Food feature images of him and other CIW staff signing agreements with the CEOs of fast-food companies, including Subway and Burger King. These agreements represent years of campaigning, thousands of signatures, hundreds of marches, hours of prayer, and even a documented case of corporate spying by Burger

King on the CIW and its partner organization, the Student/Farm-worker Alliance.[8]

During the evening, Gerardo had been working the phones, preparing for an action in Tallahassee to pressure Governor Charlie Crist to declare his opposition to the slavery documented in the fields of South Florida. Gerardo described how churches have connected faith with action in the Campaign for Fair Food. "It's hard to understand what to do in support if we don't understand each other first," he said. "It's different to hear a story directly from the workers, speaking in your church to people of faith. That story can make you believe that change is possible."

Gerardo expressed confidence in the momentum that will transform an entire food system, an unthinkable possibility to many Americans, who are accustomed to the strong role of corporations in their daily lives. "We are trying to change the system completely, and that's hard for people to grasp," he said. In conjunction with churches and students, the CIW has transformed "one of the poorest, most politically powerless communities in the country"[9] into a group that is shifting power structures, redefining sustainable food systems, and negotiating with governors, CEOs, and leaders in the food justice movement. According to Gerardo, the human rights abuses move people of faith to realize that they, too, can change an entire system.

The posters on the community center walls reflected how the CIW has used the marketing success of fast-food corporations as a tool for dismantling a powerful system built on the abuse of farmworker labor. One bright banner on the walls depicted the Burger King logo with a blue sphere and a white hamburger bun. But the words "Exploitation King" replaced the words "Burger King." Underneath this new "brand" were the silhouettes of farmworkers carrying buckets of tomatoes under the heading "Burger King exploits farmworkers."

Even with no knowledge of the Campaign for Fair Food, an audience could look at the banner and understand the message from the CIW: food from Burger King comes from exploited workers. Indeed, at the standard rate of forty-five cents for every thirty-two-pound bucket, workers would have to pick an almost impossible 2.5

tons of tomatoes *a day* to make the federal minimum wage.[10] The scale of the fast-food contracts has the power to push down the price of tomatoes, with a negative impact on the farmworkers.[11]

The CIW believes that consumers are the most powerful force for creating systemic change. In its collaboration with faith communities, the CIW maintains that consciousness passes through generations and across borders, grows slowly but never stops growing. "Consciousness plus commitment equals change," Gerardo said.

It was late that night at the community center, but Gerardo planned to continue working, making phone calls, setting up the direct action that would ultimately propel Governor Crist to denounce the cases of slavery. While Gerardo made phone calls, a group of farmworkers gathered around a white banner with paintbrushes in their hands and jars of watercolors on the table. Romeo Ramirez from Guatemala and three other workers were painting colorful signs to use in the Tallahassee march. Previously, Romeo went undercover to help authorities build a case against a labor contractor suspected of illegally detaining workers, and he received the Robert F. Kennedy Human Rights Award for his work investigating slavery charges.

He has taken his message to churches across the country to build partnerships with faith communities. "When we are near company headquarters, like Yum Brands in Louisville, it's hard because there are people from the company that attend these churches," Romeo said. "Then we do a program in that church, and the people hear testimony and realize the gravity of the human rights violation[s]. Corporations have influence, but people also realize they have to be a part of making change happen." These visits to churches by CIW farmworkers have proved critical to involving the religious community in this movement, which began in the early 1990s when the farmworkers convened their first meetings at Our Lady of Guadalupe Catholic Church in Immokalee.

Outside a small office in the back of the CIW community center, farmworkers returned from the fields in the afternoon and played the marimba, a traditional instrument from Guatemala. The marimba stood outside the back windows of the office of the nonprofit Interfaith

Action of Southwest Florida, which shares space with the Student/ Farmworker Alliance. With the backdrop of this music, the two staff members of Interfaith Action worked on laptops, sending e-mails and memos as they organized faith communities for the action in Tallahassee, which would include a silent theater piece depicting the latest case of slavery.

For many people of faith, working with the CIW has transformed both their faith in God and their belief in the potential to change the world for good. With a short brown bob and wire-rimmed glasses, Brigitte Gynther, the director of Interfaith Action, organizes churches in support of the CIW's work. "When you hear the workers' story, it connects to your faith," she said. "If you are Christian, it's hard not to consider the teachings of Jesus in these stories." Brigitte described congregations in solidarity with the farmworkers, working toward outcomes that many people of faith could not have imagined before their participation in the Campaign for Fair Food. "When we launched the Taco Bell boycott, people said they wouldn't listen to us," she remembered. "But doing what is right is the right thing to do. That is faith—having faith in humanity."

With the leadership of the nonprofit Interfaith Action, churches come to Immokalee for an "immersion visit," where workers speak about the CIW, the life of farmworkers, and the slavery rings, and then take the church members on a walking tour of Immokalee to see the housing situation. Interfaith Action coordinates about twenty-five immersion visits a year for churches and also visits at least a hundred churches each year. Individual congregations involved in the coalition's work have written letters and postcards, as well as shareholder resolutions, and provided lodging and food when workers travel to shed light on the abuses in the fields.

Now, the CIW and Interfaith Action are turning their attention to the grocery store industry, after a landmark agreement with Whole Foods Market; the targets for this Campaign for Fair Food include Kroger, Publix, and Stop & Shop. For the campaign targeting grocers, people of faith will have the unusual opportunity to influence the big-box grocery stores where they buy food on a weekly basis for their homes, their congregations, and their outreach ministries.

The Power of Religious Rituals and Prayer

A picture in the CIW media archives showed an Episcopal priest at a candlelight prayer vigil with his arms around a young Latino farmworker. When CIW members visited churches, prayer became a vehicle of connection and communication between two groups: farmworkers and local churchgoers. Jordan Buckley, the other staff member of Interfaith Action, described to me a meeting with the Northern Naples United Methodist Church's men's group, about fifty white retirees who meet weekly for an early morning breakfast. When the pastor asked Jordan to give the opening prayer, he deferred to Oscar, a CIW member and farmworker. "Oscar gave this beautiful prayer, which I interpreted," Jordan said. "Here was this man from an indigenous community in Guatemala offering a gorgeous prayer that moved this group." This prayer group reflected a connection between two worlds of faith: one of the poorest communities in the United States with one of the fifty richest counties in the United States.

It may be hard to imagine secular environmental groups like Greenpeace or the World Wildlife Fund holding prayer vigils in local communities for the protection of public lands or wildlife. But the involvement of churches with the CIW has allowed prayer and other religious rituals to take a leading role as an organizing strategy, in conjunction with the tactics of popular education, such as theater, song, dance, and brightly colored visuals, used in the coalition's work. The weekend before the direct action in Tallahassee, Florida, CIW members and Interfaith Action staff spent Sunday visiting churches, giving talks during services, teaching Sunday school classes, and engaging the support of religious groups.

As another example of this integration of prayer, St. Columbkille Roman Catholic Church in Fort Myers each year uses the "Beatitudes of the Farmworkers," combined with compelling photos of farmworker hands and faces in South Florida, to connect parishioners with the work of the coalition.[12] As Jesus states in the beatitudes of the New Testament, "Whatsoever you do to the least of my people, make no mistake, you do it to me." In each of these cases, religious rituals are seen as an asset for the cause, not a liability. Prayer provides a moment of focused hope to galvanize people into collective action.

The images around the CIW community center reflected this synthesis of popular education, leadership development, and powerful protest actions with prayer from the religious partners (fig. 1.2). The banners depicted workers holding up their fists and shouting, "¡No mas abusos!"; newspaper articles showed strikers ending a fast with a blessing by a Catholic bishop and a caricature of the Burger King with a sneer on his face. Other posters showed the positive outcomes of the campaigns, such as one with the logos of Taco Bell and the CIW with the statement "Working together for social responsibility."

Many of the original members of the CIW brought with them organizing experience from their home countries of Haiti, Mexico, Guatemala, and El Salvador, which they fled to escape human rights abuses.[13] Founders of the CIW were trained in the participatory tools of popular education, a method of education and organizing using drawings, video, stories, and theater to capture and then reflect on reality within a community.[14] In addition, the founders were

Figure 1.2   The Coalition of Immokalee Workers uses colorful artwork, song, and theater to advocate for fair food. Photo by the author.

familiar with the religious philosophy of liberation theology, which provided a theological basis for organizing in Latin America, where church-based organizing fits the context of poor, highly religious communities.[15]

The CIW has relied on aggressive protest actions to pressure corporations to provide better wages and working conditions, because the National Labor Relations Board does not protect farmworkers. Passed in 1935, the National Labor Relations Act governs relations between unions and employers and provides the right to form unions, but it excludes farmworkers and domestic workers. (At the time, farm and domestic laborers were almost all black, and southern Democrats would not support the act unless those labor groups were excluded.) In light of this injustice, the CIW turned to organizing strategies such as protests, fasts, and theater. The CIW organized, for example, a 240-mile march across Florida, a national boycott of Taco Bell, and a hunger strike in front of Taco Bell headquarters, and religious communities provided food, shelter, and prayer. While church vestries could take years to decide to stage a protest, the hospitality committee of almost any church could organize a potluck supper and lodging for workers, as well as opening prayers of reconciliation, within hours.

Churches as Partners in Justice, Rather than as Givers of Charity

As a grassroots organization, the CIW sets the priorities, with support from partners like churches and students, to create a new model for leadership development. "This is not us as Presbyterians being the experts, us doing charity work, or us doing advocacy," said Rev. Damico of the Fair Food Campaign of the Presbyterian Church. "We are partners within a movement that is bigger than the religious community." She described the partnership with the Hebrew word *hesed*, which means "loving kindness." "Where you will go, I will go," she said.

This power of partnership can be transformative, for both the church and those in need. "We as the church rarely see ourselves entwined as equals with people who are in severe poverty, but we are true partners in this case," said Rev. Damico. A CIW paper detailing the movement's history describes the relationship between the coalition and churches as true allies, with people of faith fighting with their own resources and for their own interests, standing shoulder to shoulder with the workers, rather than being passive supporters.[16]

Both CIW staff and other people of faith spoke about the position of the church as a partner for justice, rather than as a giver of charity. Many faith leaders noted that both justice and charity have their places. Justice promotes social change in institutions and political structures, while charity provides direct services, such as clothing and food. The Christians involved in the CIW campaigns recognized that, if a tomato picker works six days a week for ten hours a day and cannot afford to pay rent, something is wrong. People described the image of walking together along a path shaped by the farmworkers, who best understood conditions in the field and the possible solutions.

The First Presbyterian Church of Hollywood, only ninety miles from Immokalee and fifteen miles from the Fort Lauderdale airport, reflected one type of partnership for justice with the CIW. The church bordered two worlds, with Lexus cars and manicured lawns to the east and a transient population and lower-rent apartments to the west of the sanctuary. Hollywood Boulevard, the address for First Presbyterian, looked to me like quintessential Florida—pastel-colored stucco homes and tanned seniors driving convertibles. The congregation saw itself in the borderlands, a place to "draw together people who have been blessed with those who are struggling," said the Reverend Kennedy McGowan.

On Christ the King Sunday, the week before a march on the Burger King headquarters, Rev. McGowan preached a memorable take-home message to "have it God's way." His sermon on Luke 1:68–79 made the connection that, ultimately, God wins, even in a world where we regularly hear that power and wealth prevail. Using the CIW workers as an example of God's love, he described how Yum Brands finally agreed to the penny-per-pound increase.

"After the first year, the president of Yum Brands realized something," he said. "Not only could they afford a penny more, but it felt really good to do it. . . . You can act with love and justice toward people who need it, and still win in the marketplace. The marketplace doesn't have the last word. Jesus does." In his sermon, Rev. McGowan invited the congregation to join in the march, write a postcard, help with logistics, and let the truth set free Burger King to have it God's way.

In the pastor's office overlooking Hollywood Boulevard, Rev. McGowan reflected on the power of "being God's good news," the stated mission of First Presbyterian. "If you stand up for what's right, there is an unknown wild card—the presence of God," he said. "This work was a reaffirmation that when you answer God's call to stand up, you will be going where God is already working." Rev. McGowan believes that the Campaign for Fair Food became bigger even than the CIW, as the movement became a greater force—"a God thing"—with the involvement of so many people working for human dignity.

Many faith leaders have partnered with the CIW by representing their religious traditions in delegations to speak with executives of corporate America. "Economic justice is where the rubber meets the road in the Bible," said the Reverend Frank Corbishley, rector of the Episcopal Church Center on the urban campus of the University of Miami. "As I've become an activist, I've come to believe that justice is more important than charity. The more justice there is, the less need for charity." With other clergy, he led several delegations to Burger King headquarters and met with executives, including the vice president of public relations, Steve Grover, who made online posts bashing the CIW from his daughter's e-mail account.

Faith leaders continued to send delegations in the summers of 2006 and 2007 and to participate in protests in front of the Burger King headquarters. Many of these protests were small, but they reminded Burger King that the churches and the farmworkers were not going away. These actions culminated in a nine-mile march on November 30, 2007, to the site of the Burger King headquarters. During the march in Miami, police rode on bicycles with the hundreds of farmworkers, pastors, priests, students, and senior citizens walking in peace to demand human rights. Ultimately, the actions resulted in an agreement with Burger King to pay the penny-per-pound increase.[17]

The Church as a Place for Reconciliation

"I'm supposed to be on the golf course right now," said Edy O'Brien, as her husband, Tom, maneuvered his wheelchair into the church office. With his tanned skin, bright white hair, and blue eyes, Tom O'Brien's face drew attention away from his legs, which ended at his knees. Edy continued talking as Tom positioned his wheelchair in the tiny office. "But it's really hard to say no to this church staff. You just want to be involved." This couple appeared to be in a love affair with their church and the mission of social and environmental justice. Tom had stopped going to church for decades, until his wife joined St. Columbkille Roman Catholic Church in Fort Myers and convinced him to hear a sermon from Pastor Joe Clifford. "He hasn't missed a Sunday since," she quipped.

Given the migrations of Fort Myers snowbirds, St. Columbkille ministers to a spring attendance reaching 6,000 on Easter Sunday and a smaller turnout of 900 in the humid summers. Each week, the congregation meets in a modern sanctuary with a burnt-orange metal roof and spouting water features at the entrance. Edy described her encounters with the "pickers" in Immokalee during an immersion visit as a part of the Just Faith curriculum, a thirty-week educational program focused on faith and justice in the Catholic Church.[18] "We went to Immokalee and took a tour and then learned about their work," Edy said. "And I was holding hands with a picker. I've never known a picker. One of the pickers said a poem that was just beautiful. And there we were in a circle holding hands."

The Just Faith program includes reflection, prayer, action, and "border crossings," encounters in which church members work in an unfamiliar setting, often a cross-cultural experience in their own community. The curriculum asks participants to address questions like: What does our Catholic tradition call us to do in faith and justice?

What does Jesus call us to do? The border crossing in Immokalee was the beginning of the couple's involvement in the Campaign for Fair Food through the Catholic Church.

Tom began to organize boycotts and rallies against Burger King in collaboration with the CIW. He recruited people from the church, made signs, and then connected with twenty farmworkers, who came armed with drums, colorful masks, and theater pieces. For publicity, he called the local TV and radio stations. "This wheelchair is a real magnet for publicity," he said, shaking his head. "We did three different protests at Burger King. We were given this opportunity through the church, which encouraged me at every turn." Seventy years old, Tom said that, until he came to St. Columbkille, his only exposure to addressing real problems of the world through the church was by tithing. "I never saw the results," he said. "After the Just Faith program, you become a part of it. What would Jesus do? You are hands-on, going to Immokalee, organizing a protest." For both Edy and Tom, the church became a place of encounter, a sacred space that brought together middle-class retirees and farmworkers, all working for justice.

For their presentations to Sunday school classes, CIW members and Interfaith Action staff take the red plastic buckets that farmworkers use for the tomatoes they pick. The staff fills up the red buckets with bags of rice until they weigh thirty-two pounds, the amount someone needs to pick to earn forty cents. At Grace Lutheran Church in Miami Springs, Florida, a worker gave this lesson to the congregation, which hosted the farmworkers in the church social hall for meals during a rally at the Burger King headquarters.

A social ministry board member described watching the faces of the young boys in the church, when the CIW members asked the church youth to try to pick up the red bucket. "The children of the church were shocked to hear about slavery so close to their home," she said. "That demonstration with the buckets made quite an impression on them." The pastor of this church took his seventh- and eighth-grade confirmation class to Immokalee for an immersion visit, so they would have another encounter with the words of Jesus and justice.

For the CIW, this sacred space for healing proved critical to the success of campaigns like the Taco Bell struggle. In a letter to the Presbyterian Church (USA), Gerardo Reyes-Chavez wrote about the healing role of the church:

> The church was absolutely necessary in this struggle because you have a lot of power especially in the eyes of the corporations. And you had more connections with their human side. Executives of corporations are members of congregations. And farmworkers are church people also. Your ability to connect both with executives and with farmworkers as people of faith, allowed a point of encounter between worlds that were in conflict but were able to find, in this case through the church, reconciliation.[19]

Human Dignity as a Critical Component of Sustainable Food Systems

Upon entering a store like Whole Foods Market, a consumer finds bright produce, posters depicting the faces of farmers, and samples of foods such as fresh salsa with cilantro and organic tortilla chips. The marketing images of the sustainable foods movement focus on the conservation of small farmlands, the relationship between grower and consumer, the health benefits of organic food, the lack of conventional pesticides, and the smaller carbon footprint of local foods.

But just because food is organic doesn't mean it wasn't picked by slave labor. Organic certification provides standards for the food but not for the workers who pick that food. There is no place in a sustainable food system for salsa made with tomatoes picked by workers held against their will or forced to rely on charity despite working sixty hours a week. A systems approach considers all the factors involved in getting food from the farmer to the consumer. The American Public Health Association defines a sustainable food system as one that provides healthy food to meet current food needs while maintaining healthy ecosystems that can also provide food for generations to come with minimal negative impact to the environment. A sustainable food system also encourages local production and distribution infrastructures and makes nutritious food available, accessible, and affordable to all. Further, it is humane and just, protecting farmers and other workers, consumers, and communities.[20]

As the CIW broadens its campaign demanding the penny-per-pound increase to include grocers as well as fast-food corporations, the organization and its partner churches are reframing the sustainable foods movement to include human dignity. In 2009, the CIW coordinated a visit to Immokalee by food justice leaders from across the United States and received national media attention. The 2008 agreement with Whole Foods Market created a landmark opportunity to integrate human dignity into the language of environmental stewardship, and church leaders picked up on this language.

In a letter of support for the agreement between the CIW and Whole Foods Market, the Reverend Gradye Parsons, the stated clerk of the General Assembly of the Presbyterian Church (USA), wrote:

> Recognizing that the well-being of the earth, its resources, and humanity are interdependent, the PC (U.S.A.) believes we are called to ways of living that foster the wholeness God intends for our world. Whole Foods Market is a pioneer in crafting business practices that uphold standards of environmental and animal welfare. Through this agreement with the CIW, the company now adds new and necessary standards for human rights to its sustainable business practices.[21]

The letter calls this agreement a significant advance for a more just and sustainable food system and calls on the Florida Tomato Growers Exchange (FTGE) to "repent" and cease obstructing the penny wage increase from getting to the farmworkers. The FTGE is a lobbying group for major growers in the tomato industry. This group pressured growers not to comply with the wage increase agreed upon by fast-food companies like Yum Brands and grocers such as Whole Foods. Since that time, East Coast Growers and Packers, one of Florida's largest tomato growers, left the FTGE and agreed to implement the wage increase and code of conduct. (When the FTGE obstructed the exchange of these funds, the monies went into an escrow account. The CIW's ongoing strategy is to build enough pressure from buyers to force the FTGE to consent.)[22]

From Presbyterians to evangelicals, the religious communities that partner with the CIW have picked up on this issue of justice in sustainable foods. Stephenie Davis, a twenty-two-year-old from the evangelical First Assembly of God in Gainesville, Florida, has coordinated service trips with youth to work with the CIW. The First Assembly of God has taken about twenty-five trips to Immokalee, and these mission trips also include time in an Immokalee neighborhood called Farmworker Village, where they pray with residents and play with children. "Jesus saw needs and met them," said Stephenie. "How we treat people reflects how we treat our environment. If we lock people up in a U-Haul trailer, that reflects how poorly we treat the environment around us." Despite the diversity of beliefs among different denominations in the United States, churches agree on the fundamental need for human dignity.

Protecting Human Dignity as a Ministry: Lessons Learned

My encounters with people of faith, including workers in the fields in Immokalee, clergy at the University of Miami, and retirees in Fort Myers, all point to concrete lessons as religious communities work for human dignity in the agricultural systems that provide our food. Giving thanks to God also means giving thanks for the workers who pick that food and working for justice for all God's people. For churches seeking to expand their ministry of human dignity, these lessons provide guidance for that work.

Maintain faith in the improbable.

Christian faith is based on belief in the unknown and seemingly impossible. Yet, too often, we forget about the unimaginable, placing most of our faith in calculated plans and strategic time lines. As Christians working for human dignity, we must remember our faith in miracles, our understanding that God's love can transform reality in ways we cannot foresee. The story of the church and the CIW depended on this faith in the improbable: an organization of 3,500 immigrant farmworkers *could* forge agreements with the giants of the fast-food industry.

Integrate religious rituals and prayer into the tactics of grassroots groups.

When a campaign embraces our spiritual values, prayer and other religious rituals can strengthen our work, providing texture and meaning to the fight for justice. The leaders in the CIW were not afraid to ask religious leaders for their prayers at marches, fasts, and rallies. In this partnership, prayer provided a grounding force for those engaged in the work of protecting human dignity. For the people of faith involved in the Campaign for Fair Food, prayer drew them into the presence of God, with what Rev. McGowan called "the unknown wild card," the transformative power of God.

View the church as a partner in justice, not just as a giver of charity.

While both charity and justice have their places, this story of the church and the CIW reveals the importance of standing shoulder to shoulder with grassroots groups and letting those who have the experience in the agricultural fields set the agenda. The concept of "where you go, there will I follow" puts the emphasis on the relationship between partners, rather than on the goal. The focus on justice ensures that the church is addressing structural systems of power that oppress people, rather than merely providing charity.

Recognize the church as a place of encounter and reconciliation.

Since 78 percent of the U.S. population identifies as Christian, the church has the potential to work as a sacred space for encounter in numerous conflicts or attempts to bring healing and peace to the earth, from an environmental as well as a social perspective. People of faith exist in almost any sphere of life, just as many of the farmworkers and executives of Taco Bell were practicing Christians. Recognizing this role and the inherent power in the sacred will enhance the possibilities for the ministry of protecting human dignity and the earth.

Define the human dignity of farmworkers as a critical component of sustainable food systems.

The work of the church to protect the human dignity of farmworkers remains critical to the definition of sustainable food systems. The human dignity of workers is also an environmental issue, deeply connected with our care for the earth. Systems are not sustainable, in God's world, if they degrade other human beings. This perception has the power to transform and reshape how we view the systems that provide our food.

On Reflection

For four months after visiting Immokalee, I couldn't eat a tomato. I waited to eat tomatoes until the summer, when I could pick them off the garden vines around the campus of Warren Wilson College, my home in North Carolina. When I saw a tomato in the grocery store, I saw the face of Romeo Ramirez, who went undercover to expose the slavery rings in South Florida's agricultural fields.

In 2006, I took a group of students to visit Immokalee as part of a class on Ecology and Leadership in the Everglades. On this trip, we took an immersion tour, getting a glimpse of the dilapidated trailers that rent for exorbitant prices. We rose at 4:00 a.m. to bear witness to the workers looking for a day's wages at the parking lot, where buses lined up to transport the pickers for that day. When I lived in Central and East Africa as a Peace Corps volunteer and then as a graduate student, I had the experience of living in a community with substandard housing. But it was a different experience to travel only thirty miles from Naples, Florida, to reach one of the poorest communities in the United States.

I grew up in a family in which faith and food were one. My grandfather, an Episcopal priest, grew tomatoes in his backyard even when he could no longer see the vines to pick them. He could feel their plumpness and knew when the fruit was ripe. Growing up, we would give thanks for the food. Our family still uses my grandfather's blessing, reserved for special occasions: "Blessed art thou, O Lord our God, who has given us life, who sustains us in life, and who has brought us to this Happy Day!" And my children rely on the standard, "God is great, God is good. Let us thank him for our food."

In each blessing, the focus is on the food, but the story of churches and the CIW puts the focus on the human dignity of those who produce that food for us. I involve my students each year in educational campaigns focused on local food, such as teaching cooking and gardening classes in elementary schools. My encounters with people of faith involved in the Campaign for Fair Food reshaped my own conceptions of sustainable food systems. I will never think about sustainable foods, or a simple food like a tomato, in the same way.

Likewise, this encounter gave me more hope than ever before in the power of partnerships with the church. Churches haven't always been known for fast action. As Rev. Damico said, "In the Presbyterian Church, we're better known for forming committees to form committees." But this partnership had revolutionized the people of faith who spoke with me, in turn transforming their own religious institutions and ministries. Most of the church members I interviewed had never been involved in a campaign with so many concrete outcomes, one that made visible the power of their participation and their prayer in the face of corporate America. If the hundreds of thousands of grassroots environmental and social change organizations across the world could harness the power of the church when their missions are compatible, the result could be transformative.

Feeding the Hungry

Gardening for God's Children

When you reap the harvest of your land, you shall not reap to the very edges of your field, or gather the gleanings of your harvest; you shall leave them for the poor and for the alien; I am the Lord your God.

—Leviticus 23:22 (NRSV)

The health issues facing this community are vast and deeply connected to the available food. So feeding becomes a health issue, a youth empowerment issue, a body image issue, and an economic issue in this Harambee neighborhood. Healthy food is a right.

—Pastor Steve Jerbi, All People's Church, ELCA, Milwaukee, Wisconsin

After services at All People's Church in the Harambee neighborhood of Milwaukee, Wisconsin, parishioners headed to the back of the sanctuary to pick up radishes, basil, green onions, parsley, and other vegetables grown in the church garden. The back of the church functioned like a farmers' market, but the food, grown by youth in the church, was free (fig. 2.1). Pastor Steve Jerbi believes in the central role of food in the ministry of Jesus. "In the big picture, God uses food to connect with the people, just like manna in the wilderness and the garden in Genesis," he said.

Each Sunday in congregations across the country, the church feeds people, holy food for holy people. In a symbolic act, the sacrament of communion elevates feeding to a spiritual encounter. Priests and pastors repeat these words: "This is my body that was given for you; do this in remembrance of me." The Eucharist is the most common ritual in Christian churches, and grace before mealtimes remains the most common prayer in the world.[1] For many children in the United States, the first prayer they learn is the classic "God is great. God is good. Let us thank him for our food." In the end, as in the beginning, God and food are bound together.

The Bible includes countless references to food, including eating, planting, and harvesting, and commands to avoid eating specific foods, such as the fruit from the tree of knowledge in the garden of Eden. Some of the most classic biblical stories involve feeding: Jesus feeding thousands with five loaves and two fishes, God feeding the Israelites with manna in the desert, and the wedding at Cana. In the Bible, as in prayers of thanks, God is the provider of food, which gives his people strength to do his work. The words from the Lord's

Figure 2.1 At All People's Church in Milwaukee, Wisconsin, the back of the sanctuary becomes a free farmers' market with produce from the church garden. Photo by the author.

Prayer, "Give us today our daily bread," invoke the power of God as the source of all food.

Sharing food within the congregation is a ministry that reflects the essence of community in churches. Christians share potluck suppers and Lenten pancake breakfasts, and the ubiquitous coffee hour after services revolves around drink and often food. When someone dies, people in the church minister to the family by bringing casseroles, fruit plates, dinner rolls, and pies. Indeed, a study conducted by the Gallup organization found a correlation between parishioners' satisfaction with a church and eating together. According to the *Mennonite Brethren Herald*, 77 percent of church members who were highly satisfied with their congregation had eaten a meal with others in the church.[2]

Feeding the hungry in the wider community has long been a ministry of Christian churches, which stock food pantries across the country. In her book *Take This Bread*, Sara Miles presents the story of how her first communion at age forty-six propelled her into a lifetime ministry of feeding people.[3] At St. Gregory's Church in San Francisco, she started a food pantry that operated in the sanctuary of the church, with food stacked around the altar. For Miles, feeding others became an extension of how God feeds his people each week at the altar. All were welcome at the table, those who had food in their homes and those who did not even have homes.

In the Bible, as in today's world, food and power share a strong connection.[4] Those controlling the sources of food have power in the Bible, as in the book of Ruth, when just landowners were expected to leave grain in the corners of their fields for the poor. Access to quality food in urban areas often involves access to power. Many low-income neighborhoods throughout the United States have no grocery stores; residents' only options for food are fast-food chains and convenience stores. Middle- and higher-income neighborhoods, however, boast traditional grocery stores like Kroger, high-end organic markets such as Whole Foods, and weekly farmers' markets offering fresh, local produce. Access to fresh, healthful food becomes an issue of justice, as well as an environmental issue.

The sustainability of our food systems reflects our own health and the state of our environment. In the United States, most food travels an average of 1,500 miles from farm to plate, reflecting the unsustainable consolidation of a monolithic corporate agricultural system that depends on pesticides to grow foods and fossil fuels to transport the foods. Indeed, 20 percent of the energy used to produce food in the United States is expended *after* the harvest of food.[5] As Wendell Berry writes, eating is an agricultural act.[6] And thus, eating is also a political act. The biblical scholar Ellen Davis points to the ancient politics of eating and agriculture. She believes that the prophetic movement in Israel in the ninth and eighth centuries BCE resulted from the state consolidation of the agricultural economy.[7]

Today, as in the Old Testament, the health of the land reflects the health of God's people. Across the country, people of faith are responding to this call to integrate environmentalism into food and faith. Vineyard Christian Fellowship in Boise, Idaho, a large evangelical church, cultivates a "garden o' feedin.'" Crescent Hill Presbyterian Church in Louisville, Kentucky, a smaller congregation, maintains a garden at the church and offers a summer camp where youth produce food such as salsa from the garden.[8]

This chapter addresses the question of how people of faith have transformed the ministry of feeding by a focus on local foods, organic gardening, and equal access to quality foods for all people. The stories discovered in Milwaukee include a church where feeding is central to prayer life, the All People's Church. This chapter also spotlights a group of nuns using organic gardening for education, outreach, and prayer. The natural saints encountered along the way include Caroline Jewett, the minister of meals at All People's Church, and Sister Suzanne Moynihan, a Catholic nun who teaches earth spirituality, vermicomposting, and food preservation to people of faith. The lessons for other churches include the spiritual act of feeding, the importance of equal access to healthful food, the use of gardening to gain life skills, the centrality of food to relationships in faith, and the power of teaching and learning about simple living through food.

The Spiritual Act of Feeding: The Church Is the People

The sanctuary in the round at All People's Church featured high ceilings, a white wooden cross painted with Spanish prayers, and a large mural depicting people of diverse ethnic backgrounds seated at a table. Hundreds of origami doves hung from the high rafters on the ceiling of the church. When I arrived for services, a young man with ebony skin and long fingers played contemporary Christian jazz on the piano, while kids banged on the African drums near the keyboard. Before the worship began, Pastor Steve Jerbi walked around the pews, steaming coffee mug in hand, greeting each person and hearing updates about their lives. He sported a goatee, shorts, Birkenstocks, black-rimmed glasses, and a stole decorated with bright green leaves for this season of Pentecost.

Pastor Steve focused on environmental theology during his seminary studies, and he brought this passion for environmental justice to All People's Church, a mission church of the Evangelical Lutheran Church in America (ELCA). The worshippers in the pews at the 9:00 a.m. service included a mix of black youth and white youth seated with white adults, black adults with black kids, and several mixed-race children with their parents. This was not a segregated congregation.

Pastor Steve began the service with a greeting, telling the congregation that he had walked into his office that morning to find a staff member collapsed in a seizure and unconscious in her chair. An ambulance took her to the emergency room, and he asked the congregation to focus the service on prayer for her and for others in need. He mentioned two or three other families, including a woman who had lost her house in a fire and another church member who had been diagnosed with breast cancer. After prayers, the music director, David Nunley, played as if he were in a sacred jazz club as he belted out the song "Sanctuary." Soon, the congregation was swaying and singing this song of prayer: "Lord prepare me, to be a sanctuary, / Pure and holy, tried and true."

For the Prayers of the People, Pastor Steve called on the church, the people, to lift up their own prayers from the pews. Children asked for the church to pray for their grandparents. Adults asked for prayers for their children. Pastor Steve addressed the people in the pews *as* the church: "Will the church please stand?" The church was the people. Pastor Steve took the microphone into the pews to ask members of the congregation to do the readings; this was a spontaneous request to read God's word, rather than a list of readers created months in advance. The creed that followed included these words: "We are not alone; we live in God's world. We believe in God, who has created and is creating; who has come in Christ, to reconcile and make new. We trust God, who calls us to be the Church; to love and serve others."[9] With the end of the creed, the peace began, and every one of the twenty-five people in the congregation hugged every other.

The 11:00 a.m. service included a larger crowd of about seventy, of whom about one-third were children. During the sermon, Pastor Steve mentioned that when he returned to the neighborhood this weekend after attending summer camp, he could not go five blocks without seeing a squad car. During camp the previous week, he said, a slam poet used the following line in his spoken word performance: "It's not about keeping it real. It's about keeping it right." The squad cars in the neighborhood, the office assistant on the floor, "that's keeping it real," he said. But keeping it right is not being content with that reality, he continued. Keeping it right is asking the Holy Spirit to come into this place, to make things right.

The gospel for that day featured the miracle of feeding. "Jesus had five loaves of bread and two fish," Pastor Steve said. "We think the miracle is in the feeding. Jesus tells his disciples to feed the people. Jesus blessed the food, broke it, and gave it to his disciples and said, 'Take. Eat. This is my body, which is given for you. Do this in remembrance of me.'" Pastor Steve described a feast created by Jesus with bread, fish, and 12,000 people, an alternative to Herod's excesses. "This is an alternative feast, a banquet that never ends," he said. "We are the ones to bring the bread of Christ, allowing God to use us to keep it right, not just keep it real."

This service included more music and song, including "Blessed assurance, Jesus is mine! Oh what a foretaste of glory divine." As in the early service, the Prayers of the People were truly the people's prayers. "Pray for me and my four kids. We become homeless Friday," said a woman next to me. "My son was the victim of assault Friday," said another. This was a praying church, a feeding church. Before communion, Pastor Steve reminded us, "There is only one meal that satisfies. There is one feast that we are part of, and it is a feast that will never end." At All People's Church, communion was the real meal in the church.

Access to Healthful Food in a Just Feeding Ministry

Two children, eight-year-old Dee Lee and four-year-old Doneilla, gave a tour of the "little garden" outside the church. "We work on Tuesday mornings," said Dee. "I live on First Street, and I walk here to work. We work in the garden, and then we get checks. We just let the food grow." The little garden adjacent to the church consisted of herbs, while the big garden, a few blocks away at Fifth and West Clarke streets, featured vegetables. Both gardens were part of the Kids Working to Succeed program, which went by the acronym KWTS among the congregation.

After the tour of this small garden, Pastor Steve spoke about his first year at the church and the role of the church in feeding. The building that housed All People's Church was given to the church after Epiphany Lutheran Church lost its membership of older, white parishioners, who were dwindling in numbers in the largely African American Harambee neighborhood. Half the neighborhoods around this church are in poverty, Pastor Steve said. The average household income is $24,000. The average per capita income is $14,900, for a population that is 63 percent African American, 11 percent Latino, and 19 percent Caucasian (the remaining 7 percent identifies as "other"). Sixty-two percent of residents rent their homes or apartments.[10] This mission church has "one foot in the Lutheran world

39

and one foot in the nondenominational world," he said. "Probably half our parishioners don't identify as Lutheran." As a mission church, All People's gets support from thirteen financial partners that contribute half the annual budget. The church receives about $100,000 from the partner churches, $50,000 from members, and $44,000 from grants.

Pastor Steve pointed out the wooden cross that stood in the lot adjacent to the church. The cross was the site of the original garden and the beginnings of the youth ministry program, for children between nine and twelve, which teaches life skills through gardening. The children work two to three days a week and are paid $10 a day. The Kids Working to Succeed program hires youth leaders for $20 a day, and a Lutheran volunteer oversees the program.

The church had gardened on that site under a city ordinance that allowed them to take over an abandoned lot. The original garden included raised beds, signage, a watering cistern, and the cross. In 2006, parishioners learned that the vacant lot had been purchased for development, and the city gave the church ten days to vacate. In 2007, when Steve started his work at All People's, the lot was overgrown with no signs of development. "People were completely discouraged, as they had torn down all their work for nothing," he said. "They had dismantled the entire garden—to return the plot to a vacant lot. They had even taken down the cross." During that year, city employees continued to mow the lot and told the parishioners the land would not be developed.

After six months in his new position, Pastor Steve started telling people in the church that they were going to garden again. "I honestly had no idea how," he admitted. "But I started saying that we would do it." Steve's plan was to buy the lot, and the church had the needed $12,000. For unknown reasons, the city would not agree to sell. Later, the sale became politically untenable, when a church alderman went to jail for extortion and racketeering. In telling this story, Pastor Steve raised his eyebrows with a look that revealed how the dramatic had become normal for him and his parishioners.

The church worked with Milwaukee Urban Gardeners to find another vacant lot, which they found on Fifth and Clarke streets.

During the past year, thirty children participated in the program with five youth leaders and three adults. But the church's involvement with the lot next door had not ended. "We started mowing the lot, and just last weekend we put in a prayer garden where our vegetable garden had been," Pastor Steve said. "It was an act of civil disobedience. We reclaimed the land." Parishioners painted three benches with spiritual texts, including one passage that states they were kicked off this land used for gardening. He believes this church is creating sacred spaces, reclaiming abandoned land for positive activity and prayer.

"Ten thousand meals and the love of Jesus," Pastor Steve said. "This has become a theme for us. Our youth ministry, women's ministry, couples ministry—they all gather around a meal." In this central role of feeding as ministry, All People's serves about 10,000 meals each year, including communion meals. The church even employs a minister of meals on its staff. The offerings include Sunday breakfast, a Wednesday community lunch and Bible study, a Wednesday night meal, and a food pantry on Wednesday afternoon.

In inner-city neighborhoods such as this one, access to fresh food is typically limited and often nonexistent, while there is an abundance of fast food. "The health issues facing this community are vast and deeply connected to the available food," Pastor Steve said. "So feeding becomes a health issue, a youth empowerment issue, a body image issue, and an economic issue in this Harambee neighborhood. Healthy food is a right." In downtown Milwaukee, several blocks from the Usinger's Sausage sign and the city's RiverWalk, visitors could find an expansive organic grocery store with fresh vegetables and luxuries like raspberries, Perrier water, and sushi. But across the bridge in the Harambee neighborhood, the nearest food source I saw was a Church's Chicken, not a grocery store.

To provide more fresh food, the church joined a CSA, or community-supported agriculture program, and the local co-op, funded by an ELCA world hunger grant for education advocacy. The food from the CSA is delivered on Tuesday and provides fresh, local food to use in the Wednesday lunch feeding ministry. The church also hired Caroline Jewett to work as a minister of meals for twenty hours a week. She cooks for the Wednesday meals and manages the food shelf, which provides three days' worth of groceries to people in the church and community once each month. The program was closed for one year, after some mismanagement, Pastor Steve acknowledged, but Caroline's position and the program, funded through a $16,000 grant, put one person in charge of the food, funds, and process. A separate Siebert Lutheran Foundation grant paid for the garden supplies, and the church received a health and wellness grant from this same foundation to fund a parish nurse.

Each summer, the food from the garden is harvested by the youth in the KWTS program for their families, as well as for Sunday mornings for members of the congregation. "There is a whole lot of kingdom work going on here," Pastor Steve continued. "The barbeques we do in the summer are for the ministry of hanging out. We are going to be good neighbors. When you have a grill going, the two drug houses next door to the church get real nervous. There is competition on the block." Pastor Steve explained that Dee, who showed me the little garden, and his siblings started coming to church without their parents because they knew they would get fed. Many children came to church without their parents and sat with other adults in the congregation. David Stephens, a young boy who played drums at the 11:00 a.m. service, reflected on his role in the garden with the KWTS program and in the liturgy on Sunday mornings. "I work for God and in God's garden," David said.

Pastor Steve noted that, while the church took steps such as installing energy-efficient windows, he did not see the congregation as an environmental model. "Seventy percent of our church wouldn't say we are an environmental church," Steve said. "They might say we are a feeding church or a justice church. We still serve food on Styrofoam plates." All People's Church integrated the environment into feeding and meals, a ministry that made sense for the mission of the church. To this end, the church received recognition for its Fresh Food for All ministry from the National Council of Churches Eco-Justice Program, the Lutheran Church, and the National Religious Partnership for the Environment.[11]

Growing People and Food: Gaining Life Skills
through Gardening

After church, Amanda Juedes, the KWTS director and Lutheran
volunteer, took me five blocks from the church to the garden site.
There, a bright blue, hand-painted sign identified the raised beds as
part of the KWTS Community Garden program (fig. 2.2). In this
urban gardening program, Amanda coordinated both the garden and
the youth work program, and has dealt with the inherent challenges
of starting a garden in its first year. "My last day last summer, a drunk
driver drove a car through the garden," she said. Amanda was young,
in her early twenties, with fair skin, a compassionate air, and a slightly
frazzled look, perhaps due to dealing with drunk drivers in gardens.
"We started out planting blackberry bushes, putting on organic topsoil, and using coffee grinds from Starbucks." She explained that, in
their old location, adjacent to the church, they had an agreement with
a woman next door that they could water the garden in exchange for
helping her with the water bill. But in the new location, the neighbors

Figure 2.2 The Kids Working to Succeed program at All
People's Church integrates gardening, leadership skills, and
worship. Photo by the author.

were not receptive to that arrangement. "For the first month, we had a garden, but we had no water," she said.

To transport water, the youth would load a minivan with containers of water and drive it the five blocks to the garden. Amanda sighed as she recalled the history of this garden, adding another chapter to the water saga. The University of Wisconsin's extension program supplied a spigot for a fire hydrant, but the spigot did not work. Then they got a new spigot, but the hydrant did not work, she said. At some point, the hydrant started working, and finally the young people could garden without carrying water five blocks from the church.

When Amanda started her half-time job during the summer, Pastor Steve showed her the lot, covered in grass. "This will be our garden," he said. She raised up her hands, with a show of surprise. "Okay, I thought. I've not really ever gardened, but hey!" she said. She contacted the Milwaukee Urban Gardeners, which delivered loads of dirt. She and the youth workers borrowed a wheelbarrow and built up the beds with six inches of topsoil. In the first year at this location, the garden produced tomatoes, peppers, zucchini, sunflowers, yellow squash, and green beans. As she spoke, she touched the leaves of plants with the nurturing hand of a parent. The program with the youth concludes at the end of each summer, but the church continues the garden during the year.

She explained that the four teenage leaders for the program went through a hiring process with interviews, requiring them to show up on time and answer questions about their ability to manage younger students. After one of the first days of the program, a teen leader named Donovan apologized to Amanda; he had learned what it was like to deal with younger children in the gardening program. "He came up to me and said that he was so sorry for everything he put me through two years ago when he was in the program," she remembered. Amanda had a smile on her face, thinking of Donovan's new perspective and leadership skills. "That was the best part for me of the summer, seeing him as a leader, handling very difficult situations with younger kids," she said. Each year, partner churches provide sack lunches for the kids working in the garden, and teen leaders stay after the program to discuss the day's experiences with the adult leaders.

"It is messy, this church," she said. "But this church has healed my heart and soul and mended me and allowed me to continue to work with youth. Sometimes there is more spirit and more soul amongst the people, even if it's messy and unorganized." As if on cue as she talked about messiness, Amanda opened up a binder labeled KWTS to show me warning sheets for discipline issues. With a third warning, children forfeit half the $10 payment for the day, and a fourth warning means they lose the entire amount. The funds, called "gifts," are an incentive for participation in the KWTS program.

Each youth sets up an account at the local bank, and each participant receives checks in his or her name. At the end of the summer, if they bring a statement from their bank showing that they deposited the money, the children receive bonuses. The program leaders also discuss with parents or guardians that the money belongs to the child, not the parents. The intention is to simulate a work environment within the safe space of the church, and money management is an important part of the summer program. The previous week, for example, staff took the children to the bank, and the bank manager talked to them about understanding interest rates.

"Pastor Steve talks to the kids about giving 10 percent to the church, spending 10 percent, and putting 80 percent in the bank," Amanda said. She looked around the garden to survey the beds of vegetables. "In the midst of not having any running water," she said, "it's a miracle that anything is growing." We drove the five blocks back to the church and watched the children getting ready for high-school camp. Most of them would not have the opportunity to attend summer camp without the church. Amanda ran over to an idling car waiting to drop off a child for camp. "Destiny, do you have your bag packed?" she asked, anticipating an affirmative answer. Destiny looked a little nervous but excited and hauled her duffel bag into the church. Her mother had a magnetic sign on the side of her car that read John 3:16. After Destiny left for camp, Amanda described her own dream of a farmers' market on the lot next to the church, where children could sell the produce they had grown.

Each child from the neighborhood who participates in the KWTS program must sign a contract that outlines the goals of the program:

- Unite young people with Jesus Christ through a worshipping, caring church community.
- Help young people begin to develop life skills for work, a work ethic, learn to be on time, and have a good attitude for work.
- Help young people learn banking skills, learn to save money, and start a bank account.
- Offer young people the opportunity to attend summer Bible camp.

The contract includes a requirement that each child attend worship the week before in order to work. If a youth is late for work, he or she forfeits the monetary gift for the day. The children are also expected to make a financial pledge and an offering to the church from their gifts during the summer. The program gives bonuses of $15 for any participant who has $70 in his or her bank account by midsummer. In the end, the program is growing people as well as food.

A Minister of Meals: Food as a Foundation for Relationships

"Feeding people puts the emphasis on relationship ministry," said Pastor Steve. "When you are not eating a burger on the run, you are sitting down at a meal. You are hearing stories. You are in relation to others and talking with others." Relationships in Milwaukee mean more than just interactions between people in the same neighborhood, as a history of strained relationships between races taints this city. "This city is highly segregated," he said. "So where else do you have Latinos, African Americans, and Anglos sitting down at table together?"

In the church kitchen on a Wednesday afternoon, Caroline Jewett, the minister of meals, unpacked large boxes filled with packaged food—macaroni and cheese, spaghetti sauce, cans of green beans—and placed the food on shelves in the pantry. She introduced Lavatious, a sixteen-year-old girl who was repacking frozen chimichangas into plastic bags. "Put about eight of these things into each bag," Caroline instructed, handing me a box of freezer bags and a carton of frozen chicken nuggets. "Just put enough for a family of four."

Caroline has a budget of $40 per week to shop for food at Second Harvest; other food is donated. For $12 this week, she bought a case of green beans, which she divided into portions for families. Each Wednesday, people can eat a meal from 11:00 a.m. until 12:00 p.m., followed by an hour of Bible study. The food shelf is then open for an hour after Bible study, although people getting items from the food shelf do not have to attend the Bible study. At the food pantry, families or individuals can shop once a month. The month before I visited, forty families visited the pantry to shop for three days of food.

Caroline had worshipped at All People's Church for fourteen years before beginning her job as minister of meals. She described her true gift as women's ministry, and she served as a central member of the church's women's group, the Chat and Chew, which met monthly. She explained that the contract with a CSA provides fresh, organic vegetables, which she used for cooking parts of the Wednesday meal. Many of the people who come each week to the food pantry are from the neighborhood, just as the work program in the garden attracts local youth. "In the fellowship of Bible study—people come for the people—you feed their body and their soul," she said. "If they only cared about the food, they would just come to the food pantry once a month." She opened a freezer that revealed bags stuffed with chicken tenders, chicken chimichangas, and boxed pizzas. Families signed in at a table that held a small bucket of fresh zucchini, green beans, and herbs from the church garden, to complement the other foods. Each family could take some vegetables from that box in addition to shopping at the food pantry.

Caroline reiterated the key role of this ministry of meals in the mission of the church, beyond the food pantry and the Wednesday lunches. "We're a part of this neighborhood, and the barbeques and meals [are] our ministry of being a good neighbor," Caroline said. During vacation Bible school, Caroline cooks hot lunches for the children. With an average of twenty-five kids in Bible school and twenty-five in the KWTS program, she cooks for fifty people each day during the summers. "The gardening work program is what brought me here," she said. "My children went through the work program. Now my granddaughter is in the work program, and I bring her to church with me."

At the Bible study, a woman named Andrea led the discussion. "If you keep on praying and doing God's will, your faith will grow stronger," she said. "Jesus died so he can wash our sins away. He knows we will sin. We got to do what it says in Acts 2:38. We got to repent." After Bible study, the food pantry opened, and when someone entered the pantry, Caroline asked, "Are you shopping today?" Visitors to the food pantry signed in with a photo ID and provided proof of their dependents. They then took food items, organized into categories such as pasta, cereal, fruit, canned vegetables, soups, which they placed into shopping bags. While I was there, the head of hospitality for the church, Letha Smith, went shopping. At All People's Church, those who ministered to others also received from the ministry of meals.

Teaching and Learning about Simpler Living
through Food

While Milwaukee's inner-city youth distribute vegetables in their church, Catholic nuns grow fruits and vegetables as a vehicle for education about God's earth. At Mount Calvary, the SUNSEED Eco-Education Center is an environmental education facility focused on gardening and run by the School Sisters of Notre Dame. Sister Suzanne Moynihan uses food as a connection to simpler living in right relationship to God. Books such as *Green Sisters* have chronicled the compelling narrative of how Catholic sisters in community have championed sustainability.[12]

Sister Suzanne met me at the assisted living center of the School Sisters of Notre Dame, about fifteen minutes from downtown Milwaukee, where elderly nuns addressed each other with greetings of "Hello, Sister Grace" and "Hello, Sister Helen." On the wall of the center was a framed statement that declared, "Our mission is to proclaim the good news, as the School Sisters of Notre Dame, directing our entire lives toward the oneness for which Jesus Christ was sent." In this world of nuns, Sister Suzanne, at age sixty-seven, was among the younger sisters; she was dressed in lavender slacks, a gray T-shirt, and brown sandals. Her round face was framed by light brown hair, and she had the ruddy complexion of someone who spent time outdoors.

She sat down in a chair near the entrance of the assisted living center and explained her belief that we are all connected. "We do affect each other," she said. "We are 70 percent water, and we are deeply connected. We are mostly energy. We are just on the cusp of the divine energy. Today, you and I reflect the universe connecting here this afternoon." Sister Suzanne had been a nun in the School Sisters of Notre Dame since she was twenty; involved in peace and justice work for two decades, she sprinkled her conversation with references to books she had read and speakers who have inspired her.

In 1998, Sister Mary Ann Srnka had a dream to cultivate the land at Our Lady of Mount Carmel at Mount Calvary, which was a retirement house. They had thirty-six acres of land, and she asked another nun, Sister Mary Beck, to help cultivate the land and to raise vegetables, pigs, and chickens. Seven years later, Sister Suzanne went to Mount Calvary to learn to garden and to lead sessions on earth spirituality. Sister Suzanne, a former teacher, became the education coordinator, while Sister Mary Beck became the coordinator of organic gardening and husbandry.

The three sisters founded the SUNSEED Eco-Education Center, where they reach out to Catholic and other faith communities and teach skills focused on spirituality and growing food. "We've had Catholic parishes, synagogues, UU [Unitarian Universalist] communities—they have come to us," she said. The educational programs they offer include vermicomposting, food preservation, growing foods, organic cuisine, prayer services, web of life exercises, native crafts, and earth spirituality.

Sister Suzanne got a gleam in her eye as she described one of their programs that links local food with cooking. "I called this program Garden Plot to Pot, but they made me change it to Garden Plot to Kitchen Pot," she said. "They didn't like the reference to pot." The Eco-Education Center collaborated with a Catholic school next to its property, where the primary-school students planted seeds and transplanted the seedlings to raised beds. Now, three families care for the plots in the summer. Sister Suzanne goes into the classroom to lead dramatization, songs, and nutrition lessons, and she also serves food from the garden in the school.

"Next year, I want to take the Garden Plot to Kitchen Pot program and develop slides and a manual to show teachers what we have done, with the goal of inspiring others," she said. "Anybody can build a raised bed and use it for growing food and teaching." As she talked about food, Sister Suzanne reflected on the growth in the local food movement and the connection between food and spiritual growth. "More people are beginning to raise their own food," she said. "More people realize that the food in our stores is not that nutritious. How do we use the rest of the earth to nourish our souls?" Religions have emphasized fasting and simple foods because of the spiritual impacts on the mind and body. Intention around eating creates a more focused spiritual life, she said, just as food is a symbol of the Eucharist.

"The transformation of food in our bodies—how does that empower us to be who we are in this era?" she asked. "If we take in toxic chemicals, we don't become the genuine human beings we could be. How we raise food, what food we take into our bodies is a highly spiritual act." While she talked, she often paused to greet older sisters passing by, some using a walker or cane to navigate the hallways of the assisted living center. Sister Suzanne talked about the Green Habit, a campaign that promotes sustainable living by the School Sisters of Notre Dame and includes a series on food as a moral issue through Lent.

Describing the Catholic sisters' reputation for sustainability, she said, "We live in community, so we feed each other. Our lifestyle is such that we are committed to prayer." She also explained that the feminine connection to the earth factored into their greening practices. "Our feminine energy connects to the feminine energy of the earth," she said. "Women are connected to food and the earth."

She continued to talk, as several sisters in their nineties whizzed past on motorized scooters. "We do the work we are called to do," she reflected. "I am not inspiring, but I am passionate." At my suggestion that she seemed a bit of a radical, Sister Suzanne smiled a slow grin. "Yes, I am," she said. As we passed the pictures of the Virgin Mary and the icons of Christ on the walls, Sister Suzanne left me with one parting thought: what we are doing, she said, flows from our charism, our spiritual gifts, and we are all connected.

Feeding the Hungry as a Ministry: Lessons Learned

While vastly different, the faith community of All People's Church in Milwaukee and the Catholic nuns from SUNSEED Eco-Education Center are both working to put food at the forefront of ministry and to provide healthful, sustainable food choices to people of faith. Their work points to key lessons for congregations seeking to integrate the environment into their feeding ministries.

Recognize that raising food and feeding people is a spiritual act, central to worship and liturgy.

Our worship and liturgy in churches use food as the ultimate symbol of Christ's body. In Christian life, food as a central part of spirituality begins in the Old Testament and continues in the New Testament, from the apple in the garden of Eden to the bread shared by Jesus and his disciples. Feeding people is a ministry reflected in God's command in Matthew 25:35: "For I was hungry and you gave me food, I was thirsty and you gave me something to drink, I was a stranger and you welcomed me" (NRSV). A ministry of meals is a logical place to begin integrating the environment into the life of a congregation. At some congregations, a simple change to baking whole-grain bread for communion signals that the church values whole, unprocessed food as the symbol of Christ's body. In Iowa, a group of Lutheran and Catholic churches began using local wine for the Eucharist, and after two years, the practice had spread to twenty churches.[13] Small steps like communion bread can lead to larger steps to integrate healthful food into feeding ministries. Other options for first steps include planning a Food and Faith Sunday with a liturgical focus on food and sustainable food choices.[14]

Integrate access to fresh, healthful food into a just feeding ministry.

Many low-income neighborhoods lack access to healthful food. Indeed, in many urban communities, convenience stores and fast-food restaurants are the primary options for food. Also, due to constraints of shelf life, many feeding programs rely on processed food donated from grocery stores, rather than on fresh local foods. A feeding ministry focused on justice integrates healthful local food. Gardening programs in churches provide an opportunity to focus on justice as well as feeding. One step in this direction is integrating shares from a CSA into a feeding program. Another option is using the church as a pickup location for CSA shares for members of the congregation.

Promote life skills in a faith community through growing food.

By growing food, people can learn a variety of skills that apply to the world around us. At All People's Church, the youth in the garden program gain skills such as money management and teamwork. In gardens, people of all ages and backgrounds can work on a similar task in an outdoor setting. Seniors in the church often have a wealth of gardening experience to share with younger members of the congregation. Contacts such as cooperative extension services can facilitate workshops or aid in setting up a garden. Some churches get pledges of involvement for specific tasks, including weeding, watering, and harvesting, to ensure that the congregation supports the gardening and feeding ministry.

Use healthful food to help form relationships in faith.

Eating together is a primary strategy for building relationships in churches. From Wednesday potluck dinners to Sunday coffee hours, gatherings around food provide a context for encounters between people in a faith community. Some congregations have shifted the focus of their Wednesday night dinners to center on recipes and potluck dishes featuring foods grown in the local community. Indeed, the same Gallup study that discovered the connection between satisfaction with a church and eating together also found that church members with close friendships in their churches were less likely to leave the congregation and reported a stronger faith in God.[15] Food, friendships, and faith are interwoven in vibrant congregations.

Teach and learn about simpler living through a focus on food.

All people of faith from a diversity of income levels can enhance both their health and their spirituality through a focus on growing food and simpler living. Food provides an avenue for parishioners to learn self-sufficiency and simplicity and to integrate healthful options into existing events, including hosting a local foods potluck or using organic, fair-trade coffee at coffee hour. In tight economic times, both individuals and families in a congregation have shared interests in learning skills, whether it's how to can fruits and vegetables or how to grow herbs. At St. Alban's Episcopal Church in Springfield, Missouri, parishioners operate a "cannables" food preservation project, which began with a class on canning fruits and vegetables by a county extension agent.[16] The preserved food benefits families in the parish and in the feeding ministry. In addition to concrete skills, many resources exist for discussion groups focused on simpler living from a Christian perspective.[17] Integrating simpler living into a congregation has benefits for both outreach in the community and education and reflection for parishioners.

On Reflection

In the church of my youth, the Reverend Bill Hill explained to my confirmation class that the paper-thin wafers at communion represented the body of Jesus Christ. At my first communion, I held out my hands to receive the body of Christ and soon felt that wafer touch my tongue. As a teen, I learned to swallow the wafer without looking like I was chewing gum, attempting to embody Jesus Christ while part of his body was stuck to the roof of my mouth. As an adult, I have watched churches transform the body from those thin processed wafers to the home-baked whole wheat bread that I now eat each week at my own church. I know the women who bake that bread. I've eaten meals in their kitchens. And, somehow, it's easier for me to believe that God's love is embodied in that bread. We are what we eat—so goes the nutritional mantra. Likewise, we eat the bread each week and become the body of Christ. Through the Eucharist, we are transformed so that Christ is not "out there" but in us.

During this journey to Milwaukee, one of my strongest experiences was watching families at All People's Church pick up fresh vegetables from the back of the sanctuary. Somehow, I grew up thinking that the sanctuary was separate from the realities of radishes or lettuce picked from the ground. In Milwaukee, I realized that the sanctuary, as sacred space, makes the most sense as a distribution center for real food that feeds real people.

Every day I recognize my own privilege by the availability of local, fresh foods in my neighborhood in North Carolina. As I biked through the Harambee neighborhood, I was cut off from those options to purchase fresh food. I saw four different places to buy chips and soda, but no place to buy fresh produce. This journey made me realize that churches are in a unique position to address this ministry of feeding. No one feeds more people than the church. Churches organize food banks, feeding ministries, and phone trees to deliver

millions of meals across the country every year. At the food shelf at
All People's, the majority of the food was processed—canned beans
and chicken tenders—but the fresh vegetables from the garden and
the CSA represented an important step in enhancing access to quality
foods for all people.

During my layover in the Detroit airport, en route to Milwaukee, I sat near a young Indian man in his mid-twenties who was
reading Elizabeth Gilbert's book *Eat, Pray, Love*.[18] This bestselling
book details the author's quest for spirituality and love through
whirlwind travels across the globe. I realized that these three simple
actions—eat, pray, love—also reflect the foundation of a Christian
life. We eat symbolic bread to embody Jesus Christ, which brings us
closer to God's love.

In the Charlotte airport, as I headed home, I sat next to the same
man I had seen in the Detroit airport. He was still reading his paper-
back copy of *Eat, Pray, Love*. In Milwaukee, I witnessed the connections among these three simple verbs in diverse faith communities. If,
ultimately, the church is the people, we can start by expanding access
to and education around simple, healthy eating. Indeed, we are what
we eat, pray, and love.

3

Creating Sacred Spaces

Energy Efficiency, Green Jobs, and Green Building

God saw all that God had made and behold, it was very good.

—Genesis 1:31 (NRSV)

It seemed like the best idea was to tie our biggest cost—energy—with what we care about—creation.

—Rev. Austin Rios, La Capilla de Santa Maria

Carlos Velasquez was the first senior warden to have been deported in the history of the Episcopal Diocese of Western North Carolina.[1] His church, La Capilla de Santa Maria in Hendersonville, ministers to Spanish-speaking immigrants in the mountains of North Carolina. The former lay leader of La Capilla, Carlos was a tall, lean man in his fifties, who dressed as if he might meet the president at any time. With impeccable manners, he had a dignified but compassionate air when he knelt down to speak with young children in the church. Carlos was forced to sign a voluntary departure form after applying for and being denied political asylum.

The church rallied around him. While most churches in the diocese held bake sales to fund outreach, La Capilla hosted salsa dances and sold raffle tickets for Rosetta Stone language CDs to offset Carlos's legal bills. The women of the church sold tamales in the salon, the drafty modular building that serves as the congregation's parish hall.

"It cost this faith community a lot of money when Carlos was forced to leave," said Jill Rios, director of the religious environmental organization North Carolina Interfaith Power & Light and wife of La Capilla's priest. "All that money went to our senior warden, not the church. How do you build financial sustainability in a faith community of intergenerational poverty given a broken immigration system?" For several months, the fundraising in this small church went almost exclusively toward expenses for Carlos, a church member in crisis.

La Capilla itself was a community in crisis, whose members struggled to pay their bills, avoid deportation, and support family members both in the United States and in their home countries. For this church as an institution, sustainability meant the ability to pay the utility bills, which constitute 20 percent of the church budget. For La Capilla, green building and energy efficiency provided an avenue for increasing the financial sustainability of its sacred spaces, while promoting green jobs and enhancing the connection of its members to God's creation in their new home in western North Carolina (fig. 3.1).

Figure 3.1 Parishioners created sacred spaces such as a cob oven at La Capilla de Santa Maria in Hendersonville, North Carolina. Photo by the author.

La Capilla was situated on an oasis of fifteen acres of wooded land, just off the highways and sprawl of Hendersonville, where many of its members work in construction, factories, and fast-food restaurants. Construction of this picturesque chapel began in 1923 but was halted until the end of World War II; a visible line in the stone sanctuary marked the hiatus of more than two decades. The sanctuary and bell tower were built from large gray and tan stones, which provided beauty inside and outside the church but little insulation.

The mobile home that served as the parish hall used electric baseboard heat and provided space for weekly English classes of the family literacy program, Bible study classes, guitar lessons, and the social gatherings that followed services, baptisms, and first communions. One evening during the winter at La Capilla, someone turned on the electric heat in the salon and forgot to turn it off. The heat ran all week, resulting in $500 in additional costs, the equivalent of a month's revenues from the collection plate. "A simple mistake like leaving on a thermostat shouldn't kill a community," said the Reverend Austin Rios.

A large part of the work of churches occurs in their buildings, the sanctuaries and parish halls that surround Christians when they pray, eat, grieve, and celebrate God's world. And a significant portion of the revenues collected by religious institutions goes to maintaining the facilities where people gather, so that they can then do God's work outside the walls of the church. A tour of almost any city in the United States will reveal a diversity of religious architecture, including modular buildings in shopping malls, modern sanctuaries with open floor plans, and historic wooden churches. Despite the broad range of appearances, each physical structure demands resources—electricity, natural gas, solar energy, water—and our consumption and conservation of these resources reflect our religious beliefs and views of God.

Creating sacred space is a ministry of churches that can enhance our relationship to God by integrating the care of creation into our houses of worship. Whether designing new churches or improving the energy efficiency of existing structures, churches can address the climate crisis as a spiritual practice and create stronger connections to creation and God. Architect Lorna Day writes that good space can be found between and within buildings and can make us feel a part of our community and at peace with ourselves. "A church building becomes more than the sum of its parts," she notes. "It becomes sacred space. It elevates and prepares our souls to hear God's word."[2] Green office spaces correlate to increased productivity among workers, and hospital rooms with views of the outdoors promote the healing of patients. Likewise, churches designed with the environment in mind can enhance our connection to God, while stewarding both environmental and financial resources.

The Reverend Peter Sawtell, editor of *Eco-Justice Notes*, poses this question to churches involved in any building project: "Will they hate you or love you?" In this case, "they" refers to church members fifty years in the future who will have to live with the decisions made about the building. "Will the church members of your children's and grandchildren's generation speak proudly of your foresight and wisdom, or will they curse you for saddling them with a building that doesn't work for them?" he asks.[3]

Across the United States, churches are making design decisions that support Christian theology, the environment, and the finances of the church. At St. Matthew's Evangelical Lutheran Church in Milwaukee, Wisconsin, the church installed solar panels on the roof, which will save $1,300 each year in electricity costs. Concurrent with the fundraising, the stewardship campaign emphasized a "covenant with creation" that included lifestyle changes reflecting sustainable living.[4] For existing buildings, churches have partnered with religious environmental groups such as Interfaith Power & Light (IPL) to decrease their energy consumption through programs like "Cool Congregations," an online tool that allows churches to calculate and then reduce their carbon footprint.[5]

This chapter explores how churches are redefining the creation of sacred spaces to reflect both reverence and stewardship of the earth. The stories in this chapter include the initial steps taken by La Capilla to promote energy efficiency, build a cob oven, and create a green jobs training program, and the green addition built by Pullen Memorial Baptist Church in Raleigh, North Carolina. The stories

highlight the work of IPL, a grassroots organization with state affiliates that provides a religious response to global warming by its focus
on energy efficiency, renewable energy, and climate change. The lessons learned reveal how energy efficiency and green building in
churches promote financial sustainability as well as social and environmental justice. These stories also reflect how the process of building green can serve as a model for other churches and for parishioners
in their homes and permeate the life of a church, from worship to
education, despite the challenges of decision-making with multiple
players. Ultimately, these initiatives teach us that green buildings
reflect our religious values and allow us to care for creation through
sacred spaces that draw us closer to God.

A Stewardship Campaign through the Sun

In their early thirties, Austin and Jill Rios have a reputation as a so-
cially engaged couple whose home often functioned as an ad hoc center for community organizing around immigrant rights. With more
than 1,000 friends on his Facebook page, Austin has delivered weekly
sermons in Spanish, belted out Led Zeppelin tunes on his guitar, and
spoken in support of Latino ministries at the General Convention of
the Episcopal Church. Soon after his ordination, Austin and Jill came
to this church, where children take first communion and the choir
includes an electric guitar and bass player. They made the choice to
raise their three-year-old daughter, Aja, in a bilingual world, as most
of the adult parishioners come from Latin America.

As the director of North Carolina Interfaith Power & Light (NC
IPL), Jill brought her own passion for social and environmental justice to the mission of the church. On any given day, Jill might be
found driving a parishioner to Charlotte for a deportation hearing,
lobbying state legislators on climate bills, or overseeing student
interns in her office. Through her work, she has facilitated the first
steps for La Capilla to conduct an energy audit, install solar panels,
create a green jobs program, and improve energy efficiency as a
model for other congregations.

The church started thinking about energy efficiency because energy costs were the biggest expense for this mission congregation. In 2008, the total expenses for the church were $44,000, not including salaries and administrative costs, which were paid by the diocese. The annual bill for electricity and oil was $9,000, more than 20 percent of total expenses. Unlike other Episcopal churches in the area, La Capilla's congregation did not include parishioners whose incomes would allow substantial gifts to the church: 95 percent of the adult parishioners were undocumented, lacking the visas or residency status that would make them legal residents or citizens of the United States. Yet, about two-thirds of their children were born in this country. Due to the severe economic constraints in the congregation, the total average weekly offering was about $150. That $7,200 each year did not come close to covering operating expenses. "It seemed like the best idea was to tie our biggest cost—energy—with what we care about—creation," said Austin.

Despite financial challenges, the parishioners at La Capilla brought the richness of their home traditions and cultures to the liturgy, including music and services in Spanish and celebrations of El Día de los Muertos, or Day of the Dead. This outdoor procession and worship service featured sparkling lights and prayer flags hanging in the night to honor family members who have died, especially those who lost their lives crossing the border. The sanctuary at La Capilla represented a safe and sacred space for parishioners with connections to their past and present. As Jill often said, "This is the place where I feel the closest to God." With a growing Latino population in western North Carolina, the viability of this ministry was connected to its finances and thus to energy efficiency.

When a church considers renewable energy, the biggest question and challenge often involves the costs. Jill contacted several local solar companies for meetings and site visits to review options for renewable energy as part of a larger educational program in energy efficiency. She decided to pursue the project with FLS Energy, which has begun to specialize in providing power purchase agreements that allow organizations such as churches to invest in solar energy without immediate purchase of the equipment itself.

With this arrangement, the solar company finances the cost of developing the solar capacity. In the case of La Capilla, the church will need to raise $5,000 as an advance payment, far less than the approximately $40,000 that new equipment would cost. This model works well for nonprofits like churches that cannot take advantage of public incentives such as tax credits and lack funds to purchase the equipment. (FLS Energy also created a power purchase agreement to fund solar thermal energy at Kanuga Conferences, which is described in detail in chapter 7.)

La Capilla will function as a pilot project for NC IPL to explore options for promoting energy efficiency for other churches. As a part of the project, Jill and Austin will host an energy audit "house party" at their own home to model simple energy-efficiency measures to members of La Capilla. They will conduct an energy audit for the church with the involvement of parishioners. Several church members also have submitted applications to a weatherization program that NC IPL offers for low-income homes. "God affirms that all the created world is good, and that humans have a role that is good," said Austin. "In Genesis, God tells us we have a personal investment and responsibility to the rest of the created world." These initiatives will make a public statement about the role of the church in conserving God's resources.

Promoting Justice and Jobs through Green
Building

The energy-efficiency program at La Capilla included a focus on green jobs training, critical to the work of NC IPL. During the installation of the solar panels, interested members of La Capilla will receive training and participate in the process, building their skills in this green economy. For parishioners who work in traditional construction jobs, the experience in solar installation will prove invaluable in pursuing the growing numbers of jobs in fields like renewable energy and green building. With a broader skill set, church members will become more sustainable themselves, enabling them to give back more to the work of the church, Jill said.

The green jobs component of the project addressed the real possibility of deportation, one of the most tragic and poignant realities in the church life of La Capilla. "There is a lot of uncertainty about what will happen to our parishioners, the undocumented workers in our community," said Jill. "If we can empower people with these skills, they can take these skills back to their homes in Latin America and achieve financial and environmental sustainability." The project at La Capilla included building a cob pizza oven, a skill that parishioners could use to start a pizza-making or baking microenterprise in the United States or, if forced to leave, in their home countries. In these severe economic times, many jobs have disappeared, especially in the field of construction. Church members across socioeconomic levels are seeking new skills and jobs in this green economy.[6] "People are industrious, and they are coming up with creative ways to sustain themselves," said Jill. "We want the church to be thinking in creative ways as well."

On a rainy Easter weekend, twenty parishioners from La Capilla gathered to begin building the cob oven, with the help of Tony Beurskens from the Artisan Builders Collective in Asheville. Young Latino children shoveled mud while adults gathered rocks to build an oven from the earth surrounding their church. Tony, an humble man in his early thirties with mud streaked across his jeans, led the process in an understated way, allowing the quirks of the church members to guide the building process.

The oldest man in the congregation, Don Carlos, a Colombian gentleman with a white mustache, assumed the role of resident expert, giving his opinion about the shape of the roof, the type of wood for the posts, and the dimensions of the oven. The younger men, including Chana, who lost his left arm in a factory accident, listened with focus to Tony's directions in English, which Jill translated into Spanish. Cumbia music played on a car stereo, while Austin and Jill cooked hamburgers on the gas grill outside the prefabricated parish hall. Dressed in high black boots and a tight-fitting black dress, Chayo, a young Latina, pushed the wheelbarrow while others gathered rocks and cement blocks from the woods around the church to build the oven.

Men, women, and children set the cement blocks in a tiered circle to form the outside of the oven. The plan was to build a living roof atop the oven, but before proceeding, Tony asked the group, "Do we have an interest in building a living roof?" Having worked with many community groups in green building, Tony was adept at getting buy-in from the participants, who would ultimately provide the labor and maintenance for the structures after he left.

With Jill's interpretation, Tony explained that the support for the living roof would need to be stronger than that for a traditional roof, so it could hold water and snow. He drew several options on a piece of paper and showed the sketches to the group for their review. "We could do a square roof, which would be easier," he explained. "Or a round roof, which would be more work but would fit the shape of the oven." Oso, a young man who had provided much of the labor that morning, piped up in English, "I can work!" While Don Carlos voted for the square roof, several of the women wanted to build the round roof, which seemed more aesthetically pleasing. Gathered in a circle, the group used both English and Spanish to decide upon the round roof and to discuss options for getting the wood to build the living roof.

This intergenerational event provided concrete skills for parishioners, while creating a structure that will serve as a microenterprise for the church. The following Saturday, about twenty-five parishioners, from toddlers to seniors, gathered to mix the cob—the clay, sand, and straw used for the oven. With the Spanish version of the hokey-pokey playing, church members took off their shoes and stomped through the mud, the cob oven equivalent of smashing grapes. One month later, the church held its first fundraiser by making pizza in the oven and selling slices. In the salon, teenage boys chopped vegetables for the pizzas, and families put together toppings for individual pies.

That same summer, a college intern started a garden with the youth of the church, with the goal of growing fresh vegetables to use on the pizzas. While many families in the church grew food in Latin America, as renters in the United States, they do not own land to cultivate for gardens. Now, youth have the opportunity to grow healthful foods on church grounds. The green building project addressed larger societal issues around jobs, justice, and the environment by engaging church members of all ages, including the children running around the church grounds and a young woman in black boots pushing a wheelbarrow.

Green Building as a Model for Other Churches and Parishioners

The bright and expansive parish hall at Pullen Memorial Baptist Church on Hillsborough Street in Raleigh, North Carolina, provides a stark contrast to the cramped trailer at La Capilla de Santa Maria, but both churches have worked with North Carolina Interfaith Power & Light in green building and energy-efficiency projects. On a March morning, church members scurried around the parish hall placing cloths on tables, putting yellow daffodils in vases, arranging silverware and place settings, and counting salt and pepper shakers.

What was unique about this scene was that the parish hall included a rainwater cistern, daylighting, a geothermal heating system, and a green roof, the results of a seven-year green building project designed to add both square footage and ecological sustainability to the legacy of this progressive Baptist church.[7] The luncheon would celebrate the church's receipt of an award for the green addition from both Jill Rios and the Reverend Canon Sally Bingham, an Episcopal priest and the founder and director of the national Interfaith Power & Light program called the Regeneration Project (fig. 3.2).

Bob Rodriguez, a member of the design and construction committee, was a key player in the evolution of this green building project. He attributed the success of the building to having a committed group of people to share the learning process about HVAC systems, green roofs, solar hot water, photovoltaics, a rainwater capture cistern, native landscaping, and other elements integral to building green. Raised Roman Catholic, Bob and his wife, Linda, have been leaders in the peace and justice mission as well as the care of creation mission, both key areas of focus within the church. Seated in a Sunday school classroom in the addition, he said, "I'd never built a building before, so I was concerned about what I could bring to the table. But I just started my own personal education about green building."

Bob and Linda went to green festivals in San Francisco and Washington, DC, to hear green architects and builders speak. He took a class at Duke Divinity School in greening sacred spaces, a two-day seminar that covered the nuts and bolts of building, as well as the spiritual value of sacred spaces. When he traveled for his work in the sales of test and measurement tools for the wireless industry, he studied LEED-certified buildings, read architectural journals, and observed buildings with daylighting, light shelves, rainwater catchment systems, and green features. (LEED is the Leadership in Energy and Environmental Design program, which provides standards for environmentally sustainable construction.)

"We decided at the church to be as green as possible in the design and construction committee. 'As green as we can be' was our motto," he said. As a committee member, Bob's strategies included showing prototypes, alleviating fear among church members, and helping people to realize that green building had been done before.

Figure 3.2 Pullen Memorial Baptist Church received a green building award from Interfaith Power & Light in recognition of the green addition to its church. Photo by the author.

Part of his research for greening the church involved applying these principles to his own home, where he and his wife installed a solar water heater, replaced an old heat pump with an energy-efficient one, and weatherized. They also added a 1,700-gallon underground cistern in conjunction with eight rain barrels to collect rainwater for their organic garden and decrease demand on their own well. This green feature was especially timely during the 2007 drought when many of their neighbors' wells went dry.

The design and construction committee came up with a plan that went first to the deacons and then to the membership for a vote. "We had to think about the triple bottom line—the social, environmental, and economic costs of the building—the three components of sustainability," Bob said. He distributed materials to members of the congregation that explained why the environmental choice made the most economic sense. A geothermal system, for example, would save $6,000 a year, but it cost $170,000 more up front. The system would save $300,000 over 50 years. "If we can save money to do more of the mission work of the church, [can] someone explain to me why we should not do this?" he asked. Pullen already had a strong commitment to social justice, and this project extended that work to the environment, while saving the church money in the long run.

"You can build with less money, but if the carpets, paint, and building make you sick, is it worth it?" Bob asked. He said that, when churches build a new structure, their members typically live with that building for a hundred years. "Don't compromise and go halfway, because you will have to live with your mistake," he said. The addition to the church will use 70 percent less energy than a traditional building because of the green features. With its 125-year history and reputation for social justice, Pullen Memorial Baptist Church now served as a model for green building to other churches facing similar decisions about additions or renovations, as well as an example to its own members.

The green addition was constructed behind the original Romanesque brick sanctuary, built in 1923, and provided relief from overcrowding in Sunday school classes, which were overflowing into hallways. The new structure also housed the nonprofit Hope Center, which ministered to the unemployed and homeless in the community and provided low-flow showers, laundry facilities, and educational programs for job seekers. The total cost of the building was $3.7 million, and a three-year capital campaign raised $2.2 million in gifts. An unexpected gift in 2008 left only 20 percent of the costs to be financed with a loan.[8]

On the day of the award ceremony, several local clergy attended the luncheon with the explicit purpose of learning how Pullen had accomplished its green addition, especially in hard economic times when contributions to churches and other nonprofits have decreased. Throughout the day, church members spoke about their role of bearing witness to environmental stewardship, both in their own homes and to other churches in their region. In some ways, the green building had become part of Pullen's Christian testimony to the public.[9]

Building Green Is More than an Addition to a Church

As they sat on folding chairs in the new parish hall, Pastors Jack McKinney and Nancy Petty described the process of building green from their perspective as religious leaders, charged with ministering to all in the church and being stewards of the financial resources of the institution. Mission groups form the backbone of the church, where small groups of parishioners spearhead efforts such as social justice and creation care. "At this church, when a handful of members get passionate about a mission, they can put their beliefs into action," said Pastor Jack, a tall man with clean-cut blond hair, a lime green tie, and a welcoming southern accent.

The care of creation mission group worked for years to raise the consciousness of the congregation about the importance of God's mandate to heal the earth. The mission group organized worship services around creation care and invited environmental speakers to the church. Mission members designed programming around the issue of "dominion" in the Genesis account, emphasizing that dominion means being in relationship to God's world. The group also organized movie nights focused on environmental themes. "Over time, you've got Sunday worship, Wednesday nights, Friday nights, the youth group, all thinking about the environment on some level," said Pastor Jack. "Even if you're not an environmentalist, the environment has gotten into the fabric of your church."

So when the pastors started thinking about the members of the building committee, they knew someone from the care of creation group had to be on that committee. One of their roles as pastors was to help the care of creation group find appropriate ways to educate the church about the environment, which could not include "converting" people to environmentalism through heavy-handed tactics. "The church doesn't want to feel bullied, and the care of creation group doesn't want to feel disappointed that action isn't being taken quickly enough," said Pastor Jack. "It's a balance." With a quick laugh, Pastor Nancy piped up, "People in a church can get up in arms if they think someone else in the church is trying to tell them what to eat or what to do."

In approaching green building, Pastor Jack emphasized, it is important to integrate environmental messages from the pulpit. "You've got to talk about how green building benefits the community from a theological perspective and a financial perspective," he said. "The message is about the goodness of God's world and the importance of paying attention to our connection to that world." For pastors and lay leaders, infusing the environment into the fabric of the church, into the liturgy, and into Christian education builds a foundation for green building.

Reconciling Multiple Voices and Conflicts while Building Green

For many couples, renovating a house can become a stressful process with complex decisions involving finances, aesthetics, and style. Similarly, in any church, building projects involve multiple and often competing voices from the pews. In describing the decision-making process, Pastor Jack said, "In all honesty, this story of building green at Pullen split our environmental group because of trees that had to be taken down and the size of our footprint with the building." The decision-making process for the addition included interviewing architects, conducting a space analysis, compiling membership surveys, holding a capital campaign feasibility study, creating draft designs, and, finally, putting the plan before the entire membership for a vote.

The church voted for the green design after almost seven years of planning, but then some people realized that the project would require cutting down some trees, said Pastor Jack. Three months before construction was slated to begin, a group in the church sent a letter saying that this addition was a mistake. "There's a lot of healing that has to take place," he reflected. For two months, the church had "painful internal conversations" and eventually lost some members because of the controversy. "We hope they will come back, but today, receiving this award, today was a healing moment," he said.

From a pastoral perspective, navigating different groups during a building process can be challenging. "Our job as pastors was to minister to all groups, including those who were suddenly against the project," said Pastor Nancy. "But the people on the building and construction committee felt alienated when we listened to those against the project. We had people on both sides mad at us." Pastor Nancy's advice to other churches facing a building project was to continue to put the information about all the issues in front of the congregation throughout the process. "We didn't anticipate the opposition over the trees," she said. "You have to look at all the groups and let them get their voices out. Make sure the minority voices are getting out as well. And also don't assume the majority is feeling fine, just because they are in the majority." In this case, members of the building and construction committee felt frustrated by the opposition, even though the construction had been approved by the church membership.

Pastor Nancy compared the issue of green building to people getting on a train at different stations. "You have to remember that you've got to keep going back to get people and give them the same information you've already given others," she said. "We were six years into this project before organized opposition came up. We voted, and there was no opposition. And then right before the project, we had opposition." Ironically, environmentalists were the ones who voiced concern about the green project because they were opposed to cutting trees.

The two pastors reflected on the lessons they could pass on to other faith leaders. "We may have taken too long in this process, too much time," said Pastor Nancy. From the beginning to the end of the project, the world changed. "We had 9/11, the political scene shifted, the economy collapsed," she said. "And in a seven-year period, the church changed." They both also stressed the importance of hiring an architect who understands the church's theological beliefs as the ultimate foundation for the building. Pastor Jack explained that the design committee interviewed several architectural firms before deciding on Dixon Weinstein Architects in Carrboro, North Carolina. "When we got nervous about money, they were able to help us remember our green priorities and beliefs," he said.

Once the green addition was complete, the pastors began fielding inquiries from other churches interested in sending their building committees to visit Pullen. "This has the potential to be a witness to the religious community," Pastor Jack said. "You can do this, too. It's not a fringe issue. We were out of space, and we added more space and went green in the process." Pastor Nancy chimed in on that note: "We are a welcoming and affirming church, but now, we are a church that cares about the environment."

Both pastors pointed out the reality that fewer people in the United States are going to church on a weekly basis, but more people define themselves as spiritual. "People value nature," said Pastor Jack. "So if we aren't reflecting that value, we aren't relevant to the community. If you don't know the culture of your church, you can't serve them. This culture values the environment, and this building needed to reflect those values."

Sacred Spaces That Care for Creation Draw Us
Closer to God

As she mingled with parishioners at the luncheon, the Reverend
Canon Sally Bingham gave the impression of someone who was both
approachable and direct. At age sixty-seven, she leads the Regeneration Project, the umbrella organization for the 30 state affiliates of
Interfaith Power & Light.[10] At the dedication at Pullen Memorial
Baptist Church, she reflected on the "generational mission" of helping faith communities to fulfill their responsibilities for the stewardship of creation. "At Pullen Baptist Church, the membership is
growing because of the environmental focus," she said. "If people in
the pulpit would talk about things that matter to young people, the
numbers in the church would grow." Rev. Bingham made the point
that the scientific community has been talking about climate change
for thirty years, but the religious voice brings a moral dimension to
the discussion. "Climate change is the moral issue of our time, and
clergy can have far more impact than scientists and politicians," she
asserted.

One aspect of Rev. Bingham's appeal as the director of Interfaith
Power & Light was the story of how she connected her own religious
values to issues of energy efficiency, renewable energy, and conservation. As a stay-at-home mom, she was on the board of a national
environmental organization and involved in environmental issues in
her home state of California. A lifelong Episcopalian, she wondered
why no one in the churches was talking about environmental threats.
She talked to her bishop about this void in the church and, in time,
decided to enroll in seminary, although she did not want to preach
nor lead a parish. "I just wanted to study why the church was not
responding to the environmental crisis and what we could do about
it," she said.

Before she could go to seminary, however, she needed to get an
undergraduate degree, so at forty-five, she became a freshman in
college, graduated, and then proceeded to seminary. In 1997, with
fellow seminarian, Ben Webb, she started the Regeneration Project
and now works as canon to the environment for Grace Cathedral in

San Francisco, California. "Ten years ago, it was difficult to walk into a church and talk about climate change," she said. "But now that has changed. The climate issue is about the well-being of the whole communion." As evidence of this shift, Rev. Bingham currently serves on President Barack Obama's Advisory Council on Faith-Based and Neighborhood Partnerships.

The IPL website includes YouTube clips of sermons that connect religious beliefs to environmental issues, such as green building and energy efficiency.[11] In one such clip, Rev. Bingham speaks about Mark 12:28 and God's commandment for us to love our neighbor. If you love your neighbors, you won't pollute their air and water, especially if you think of your neighbors as those who come after us, she said. Like many in the religious environmental movement, her sermons often debunk the "dominion" myth, emphasizing that dominion means to steward, care for, and love. "We have dominion over our children, but that doesn't mean we can give them black eyes," she said. "Instead, we nurture them and protect them, so they can flourish."

With its focus on climate change, the IPL website highlights Bingham's book *Love God, Heal Earth*[12] and the DVD *Renewal*, a documentary on the religious environmental movement. The site features an online store for affordable, energy-efficient products like compact fluorescent lights (CFLs) and resources for congregations, such as how to conduct a "carbon fast" for Lent and how to calculate their carbon footprint through the "Cool Congregations" calculator. Other sources include success stories from IPL affiliates across the country, as churches integrate aspects of green building and energy efficiency from California to Georgia.

To connect sacred spaces with global warming, IPL uses a model of state-based organizations for local autonomy with a national message.[13] Participating congregations in each state sign a covenant to reduce their greenhouse gas emissions, but the affiliates allow congregations to tailor their strategies to the diverse energy policies and faith traditions in each state. Each year, the directors, staff, and board members of all thirty affiliates gather in Washington, DC, for an annual lobbying day and an opportunity to network and share strategies. In

2009, the state affiliates lobbied their legislators in support of the American Clean Energy and Security Act (H.R. 2454).

One of the affiliates with the longest history is Georgia Interfaith Power & Light (GIPL), which provides programming such as energy audits for its 120 member congregations. The office is located at 449½ Moreland Ave., above an Indian restaurant and across from the Vortex Bar & Grill, a famous burger joint in Atlanta. With training as a bat biologist, Katy Hinman combines the unique educational background of a Ph.D. in ecology and evolution with a master's degree in divinity. Executive director of GIPL for five years, Katy said that the organization tries to integrate environmental stewardship in the entire faith life of a congregation, although involvement in religious environmental initiatives often begins with an energy audit. Many congregations approach the organization because of high utility bills, and then her staff brings in the theological perspective. "Once people see this as a natural part of their faith life, they can integrate it into the entire life of their congregation," she said.

GIPL works with volunteers who conduct the energy audits for congregations with the participation of clergy and a lay leader who has experience in facilities management. As a follow-up to the audit, Katy might discuss the findings from the energy audit with an adult education class, screen a film like *Renewal* or *Kilowatt Hours*, or organize a project like a CFL sale. Many of her congregations have gone into communities to swap out incandescent lightbulbs for longer-lasting CFLs as service projects.

The organization offers two levels of energy audits. Conducted by a volunteer, the basic audit addresses low-hanging fruit, like weatherization. Congregations pay a donation of between $100 and $300 for the basic audit. If a congregation wants a more detailed audit, it contracts with Southface Energy Institute, whose engineers provide a more detailed assessment for a larger cost of $2,000. Katy said GIPL has sponsored the detailed energy audits for five pilot congregations, but the level of information given back to the faith communities was often overwhelming.

"Consider an HVAC unit for a church," she said. "We know that congregations will use it until it breaks, even if they find out from an audit that the unit is an energy sink." The staff at GIPL encouraged churches to think about what changes they can make now, like lightbulbs or insulation, and then to set up a sustainability fund to save money for long-term changes. Then, when appliances break, they have the money in hand to buy the greener choice.

Georgia Interfaith Power & Light also has managed a grant program funded by the Kendeda Foundation to provide matching funds for energy-efficiency improvements. The grant provided $25,000 in matching funds, and the foundation has supported ten congregations through three rounds of funding. In the 2009 call for applications, it received twenty applications from congregations. To gauge the impacts of the improvements, the congregations had to provide two years' worth of utility bills and monitor energy bills for two years after implementation.

Katy thinks that environmentalism in the church is like the role of music in a congregation. "You don't question the integration of music into a church," she said. "That's how we need to think about the environment and churches. It becomes a 'Well, duh!' connection. We have to emphasize all the places in religious scripture where these environmental themes exist. Religious environmentalism is in our history, our traditions, our texts."

Like many faith organizations, Georgia Interfaith Power & Light screened the film *An Inconvenient Truth* in congregations across the state. Indeed, as a part of its national outreach, the film was shown in more than a half million congregations across the country. Katy was part of this unprecedented effort to educate people of faith about global warming. As a scientist and a faith leader, she saw the importance of both science and religion in creation care. "We need the science provided by *An Inconvenient Truth* as a wake-up call. But there's a difference between the wake-up call and what gets me out of bed to make a difference in the world."

The week that she screened *An Inconvenient Truth* in local congregations, Katy saw the film ten times. One morning that week, her alarm went off and she thought, "If I don't get up, at least I won't turn on my lights, drive my car, and use more fossil fuels." She realized that was not the intended effect of the movie, but she also saw that her faith propelled her to get out of bed and act.

This work has revitalized Katy's relationship with God because her faith has become more public and community-focused. "I felt my spiritual experiences that I had in the past were connected with nature but very private," she said. "Being in a scientific community, I didn't go around saying, 'Wasn't that sunset holy?' But now I feel more community-oriented in my faith. This is something I can share and can translate into action." Katy now plans to become a minister because of her work in the religious environmental movement, although she never imagined herself in this role in the past. (Indeed, in late 2009, she assumed a part-time position as GIPL regional program coordinator in order to pursue ordination in the United Methodist Church.)

She described leading a "secret double life" in graduate school when she would go to a Bible study group on Saturday nights rather than go out with her graduate school friends. At the same time, she would tell her more conservative friends at church that she studied in the Department of Ecology, rather than Ecology and Evolution. Now, these two parts of her are connected and reflected in her work, her Christian practice, and her network of friends.

Creating Sacred Space as a Ministry: Lessons Learned

The congregations at La Capilla and Pullen Memorial Baptist Church reflect vastly different demographics that share a common value in creating sacred spaces that honor God. These churches and the work of Interfaith Power and Light reveal lessons for enhancing energy efficiency and green buildings in reverence to God's earth.

Enhance the financial sustainability of churches through energy efficiency, renewable energy, and green building.

As they conduct energy audits and install solar panels, churches across the country are turning to green building as a way to save long-term costs. For the Spanish-speaking members of La Capilla, the energy-efficiency initiatives will reduce the church's energy costs and enhance the viability of a congregation 20 percent of whose budget goes to utility bills. In many states, creative financing options exist for churches to install solar panels through arrangements such as power purchase agreements or specific grants. Churches can turn to resources such as "Building in Good Faith" from the organization GreenFaith for help with understanding green building costs and fundraising green dollars.[14] Congregations should consider life-cycle analysis and assessment when comparing green building with conventional building so as to analyze both the initial cost of materials and the cost of ongoing operations as factors in the total cost of a building or renovation. Ultimately, energy efficiency and greening the facilities can promote the financial sustainability of congregations.[15]

Promote justice and economic opportunities for church members with green building and energy efficiency.

The current economy demands relevant training for green jobs, including the installation of solar panels and the weatherization of homes. When churches create or renovate sacred spaces, this work provides an opportunity to train church members for a green economy, where jobs help to address climate change. At La Capilla, the energy-efficiency initiatives incorporated green jobs training that also recognized the tenuous nature of the work environment, given the economy and the undocumented status of many of the parishioners. To that end, this project included a focus on justice and equal access to relevant job training. In an economic downturn, many churches face the challenge of providing support for the growing numbers of unemployed people in the pews. Green building provides a chance for churches to remain relevant on both environmental and economic fronts.

Create green sacred spaces that can serve as models for other churches and for parishioners in their homes.

Many Christians attend church to participate in a community that models the Christian life. Participating in outreach and service through church, for example, is a way of modeling the principle to love our neighbors as ourselves. Congregations have the capacity to teach us how to create sacred spaces that respect the environment. In the case of Pullen Memorial Baptist Church, one of the members of the design and construction committee retrofitted his own house with energy-efficiency measures as an outcome of his research for the church addition. At the dedication ceremony, pastors from other Baptist churches in the region came to learn best practices from this congregation. Churches can become models for their members on creating spaces in their homes that save money and steward the earth's resources.

Ensure that building green is not just an addition to a church but permeates the fabric of a church, including in worship and in Christian education.

Green building is not an "add-on" to a church but reflects the principles held by that faith community. Most churches that have made the decision to green their spaces have integrated the environment into the life of the church, through worship services, outreach, or education. At Pullen Memorial, the members of the care of creation mission group designed a liturgy for the creation season in the fall, organized movie nights around environmental themes, and involved the youth group in environmental stewardship. Integrating the environment in small ways into church life is a first step to greening sacred spaces.

Recognize that decision making about sacred spaces will involve multiple players and therefore the potential for conflict, but also room for reconciliation.

In decisions involving sacred spaces, churches often operate like an extended family at a holiday, with multiple agendas and potential conflicts. At Pullen Memorial, the appointment of diverse representatives

79

to the design and construction team succeeded in placing a high value on communication about the project to the church members. During the seven-year planning process, however, the membership of the church changed, and indeed, the world changed. The committee did not anticipate the opposition three months before construction began, since the church had voted to support the addition. In the end, this situation presented a chance for reconciliation and healing, a process that takes time. To facilitate decision making, the Building in Good Faith website by GreenFaith includes concrete steps for planning, including involving all voices in a representative leadership team, creating a theological mission statement, and communicating effectively and consistently.[16] The guidelines for communication include welcoming resistance as a part of achieving consensus. While difficult, this step is key to ensuring parishioners' support after the planning process.

Sacred spaces that care for creation reflect our deepest religious values.

The buildings where we pray and sing and live in Christian community should reflect our religious values and bring us closer to God. When God declared the world as good, he charged us with stewarding the earth, protecting it for those to come. To that end, sacred spaces that protect the environment reflect our love of creation. The commandment for us to love our neighbor as ourselves demands that we protect the air, soil, and water for our neighbors in our own communities and around the world. Green sacred spaces have a firm theological foundation, and successful efforts to green a church must appeal to those religious values that reflect our care for God's creation.

On Reflection

After the first weekend of building the cob oven at La Capilla, I drove home with my daughters and saw six police cars at the Days Inn near our home. The six officers surrounded one young, handcuffed Latino man. The size of the response seemed larger than the threat of one young man. While I did not know the details behind the arrest, I did know that many members of La Capilla have been arrested for driving without a license, and some have spent time in jail or been deported, as was Carlos, the senior warden. One young mother of three children had her car impounded right after she bought groceries, which she could not carry without her vehicle. What do these scenes have to do with creating sacred space?

Building the cob oven at La Capilla was a sacrament, the creation of a space of reverence. My own daughters, with their blue eyes and fair skin, stomped in the mud to the Spanish version of the hokey-pokey. I have one photo of my daughter Maya with another ten-year-old from the church, and they have painted their cream and copper faces with the muddy streaks of clay mixed with water and sand that created the cob oven.

One of my students, Amy, worked as an intern on this project. On the first morning of work, she drove down the interstate in a truck loaded with sand. When it turned out to be the wrong kind of sand, she was almost in tears, but somehow the motley crew of workers, led by Tony, made all the elements—the rocks, wood, sand, and water—work together. When Amy started the internship, she was nervous about calling parishioners and asking, in Spanish, for volunteers. But as she wrote later in a reflective paper, "I have found comfort in the realization that the people I work with at La Capilla want to be a part of these projects. They want to learn more about cob ovens and gardens and composting. . . . I am dumbfounded by how close a connection I feel to La Capilla."

For the parishioners at La Capilla, the energy audit, solar panels, cob oven, and gardens are also attempts to recreate some of the green spaces, the sacred spaces, they left back home. In turn, they are receiving new skills, teaching skills to their children, and enhancing the viability of their church. In the words of the Building in Good Faith website, they are not just creating buildings, but creating *just* buildings. We create sacred spaces that honor the earth, and somehow God's grace, the unexpected, enters into the scene.

My interactions with churches working to create energy-efficient spaces showed me that churches can mirror environmental practices and bring us closer to God. In my interviews with churches in Georgia, I saw a priest at Epiphany Episcopal Church in Atlanta pull his bike from his office to ride home after church. The other priest at this church had been an organic farmer in her former life, and the altar guild created displays of fresh fruits and vegetables to adorn the altar at her ordination service. That space is sacred.

Through my collaboration with Jill Rios at North Carolina Interfaith Power & Light, I can now envision a time when every church in western North Carolina features bold solar panels capturing the rays of God for the church. The length of time to accomplish some of these initiatives, such as the addition at Pullen Memorial Baptist Church, can be daunting. But the outcomes, in terms of energy conservation, will last for decades or longer. I also have seen initiatives, such as the work at La Capilla, become a magnet for funding and volunteer labor because the ideas seem both practical and ethical.

North Carolina Interfaith Power & Light has launched an initiative called Project Energize, through which teams of volunteers from congregations will weatherize low-income homes through simple measures, such as insulating attics and crawl spaces and repairing ductwork. A 2002 Department of Energy study found that weatherization reduced energy costs by an average of 32 percent.[17] It makes sense for us to save God's resources through energy efficiency, especially when low-income residents spend 25 percent of their incomes on utilities. To this end, we continue ministries like building sacred spaces but through the lens of the environment. With this perspective, our acts save both the earth and ourselves.

4

Responding to Natural Disaster and Rebuilding

Loss and Resurrection on the Gulf Coast

Hear my prayer, O Lord; let my cry come to you. Do not hide your face from me in the day of my distress. Incline your ear to me; answer me speedily in the days when I call.

—Psalm 102:1–2 (NRSV)

The church was the catalyst for getting things back in order after Katrina, not the government.

—Jackie Robinson, St. John Baptist Church,
New Orleans, Louisiana

Four years after Hurricane Katrina, kudzu was growing over rooftops in New Orleans as nature consumed abandoned houses, schools, and churches. When Katrina struck, televisions and computer screens showed images of bodies floating through the Lower Ninth Ward, families crammed into the Superdome, and a sea of people left abandoned on the bridge leaving New Orleans.[1] We heard voices depicting the reality of suffering amid natural disaster along the Gulf Coast. "We just need water," said a young black man in a news clip. "We can't get something as simple as water." The church was one of the first institutions to respond to this large-scale national disaster, bringing not only water but also resources to gut houses, clear debris, and rebuild churches and communities.

On Canal Street in New Orleans, First Grace United Methodist Church resulted from the merger of the predominantly black Grace United Methodist Church with the white First United Methodist Church. Before Hurricane Katrina, these two churches worshipped a mile apart from each other. The merged church now reflects the ethnic diversity of the city of New Orleans and a focus on sustainability with innovative green building techniques.

With drums and upbeat versions of traditional hymns, the music, worship, and membership reveals the integration of the black and white congregations, as well as the new Latino presence in this neighborhood.[2] "I think First Grace is what heaven looks like," said the Reverend Ramonalyn Bethley, the district superintendent with the United Methodist Church. "That's a gift from Katrina we wouldn't have had otherwise."[3] The congregation received a green award from the National Council of Churches for energy efficiency in rebuilding, as well as national attention for the relevance of its ministries in a post-Katrina world. The extent to which any church can integrate ecological, social, and economic needs into rebuilding may reflect the viability of communities in the face of climate change.

Cassandra Carmichael, director of the Eco-Justice Program of the National Council of Churches, USA, said that the church has been the first responder in natural disasters throughout history.[4] After Hurricane Katrina, denominations affiliated with the National Council of Churches gave a total of $250 million for recovery efforts. Yet the increasing rate of natural disasters will put an inordinate stress on the faith community. Trends indicate that, over the next thirty years, more than half the hurricanes will be category 4 or category 5, as a result of the warming of ocean surface temperatures. Given this prediction, the faith community would need to increase funding by more than 42 percent to maintain current levels of support. These trends are documented in a report by the National Council of Churches that examines the impacts of climate change on core church ministries such as disaster relief.[5]

"Climate change is not just something that will happen to other people," Cassandra said. "Climate change happens inside the church walls, as well as outside." Many churches and faith organizations are making the environment a priority as they respond to the increasing scale of natural disasters precipitated by climate change. Brad Powers, executive director of the Jericho Road Episcopal Housing Initiative, said, "The storm has given the opportunity, for those who choose, to enter into green activity in rebuilding New Orleans." This chapter reveals how churches are transforming the ministry of disaster relief and rebuilding by integrating the environment into their efforts.

The stories discovered along the Gulf Coast include the congregation of St. John Baptist Church, which integrated energy efficiency into their rebuilt church; a group of innovative churches called Sustainable Churches for South Louisiana; Desire Street Ministries, which rebuilds churches and educates youth; and the Jericho Road Housing Initiative, a program that spearheads energy-efficient, affordable housing. The lessons learned point to the power of hope from faith, the importance of prioritizing and coordinating sustainability among denominations, the potential of partnerships with secular environmental groups, and the long-term economic gains from investing in green building.

The Power of Hope from Faith

The rebuilt St. John Baptist Church at 8540 Panola Street was a small, neat, red-brick building on the corner of Panola and Leonidas streets in the Carrollton area of New Orleans (fig. 4.1). One mile from Panola Street, the houses on Carrollton Avenue were rebuilt, refurbished, and resurrected in the bright colors characteristic of New Orleans architecture. But closer to St. John Baptist Church, most houses that I passed were still decayed, with each rebuilt house sitting as an island in the middle of destruction. In the nearby blocks, the churches, both abandoned and rebuilt, included St. Joan of Arc Catholic Church, Rising Star Missionary Baptist Church, and Epiphany Evangelical Lutheran Church. People were rebuilding while living next to homes taken over by moss and kudzu, which were literally swallowing up the neighborhood. The black residents sitting on

Figure 4.1 After Hurricane Katrina, Rev. Don Boutte collaborated with the National Council of Churches to integrate energy efficiency into the rebuilding of St. John Baptist Church in New Orleans. Photo by the author.

abandoned porch steps around this neighborhood reflected the racial and economic divide in the rebuilding process.

The Levees May Fail, but God Never Fails Us   Inside the church before the service, parishioners greeted each other with hugs, catching up on the gossip of the week. The choir began the service with calm, quiet hymns that gained momentum as they segued into triumphant, joyous song: "Holy, holy, holy, Lord God Almighty. / All thy works shall praise Thy name in earth and sky and sea!" With this hymn of praise, the Reverend Don Boutte, with his golden skin, light brown eyes, and booming voice, entered the sanctuary in a well-fitting suit and a red tie. The responsive reading for the day reflected themes of triumph and ended with this call: "Because greater is he that is in you, than he that is in the world. All these things I have spoken unto you, that in me ye might have peace, in the world ye will have tribulation. But be of good cheer, I have overcome the world."

In the face of Katrina's disaster, choir member Jackie Robinson embodied the hope revealed in the reading that Sunday morning. Dressed in a bright pink dress, black flats, and a wig of tousled black curls, Jackie was sixty-four but looked closer to fifty. Before the service, she greeted other choir members with this simple proclamation, "Good morning, child of God!"

According to Jackie, God used churches to show us that we have the opportunity to work with each other as brothers and sisters of Christ. "The church was the catalyst for getting things back in order after Katrina, not the government," she said. Jackie repeated her take-home message that the levees may fail, but God never fails us. Pastor Boutte later said that, while Jackie lived in a government-issued FEMA (Federal Emergency Management Agency) trailer for three years, she kept the church together during the rebuilding as a self-appointed first responder of hope for other parishioners also affected by the natural disaster. Her actions revealed that the church's ministry of responding to disaster begins with the people in the pews.

Worship in a Tent and Rebuilding for Energy Efficiency　　After the storm destroyed the church, an elderly woman told Rev. Boutte that they needed to meet as a congregation, even if they had to worship in a tent in the "wilderness outdoors." In November 2005, between thirty and fifty people began to hold worship services—in a tent. "Back then, there was nothing here—no cars, no people walking—just silence," Rev. Boutte said. He described an echo of voices when the parishioners sang hymns. Thankfully, the winter of 2006 was mild, with only one day of inclement weather during the service, a weather pattern Rev. Boutte attributed to divine intervention. By January 2006, the church had received its insurance check, and a young man in the church agreed to serve as the construction contractor at cost.

As the executive director of a group called Churches Supporting Churches, Rev. Boutte helped to bring thirty-six African American churches in New Orleans into partnership with 360 congregations nationwide to provide support, training, and advocacy for the rebuilding process.[6] Through his involvement in this organization, he connected with the National Council of Churches (NCC) and Cassandra Carmichael. The Eco-Justice Program hosted workshops along the Gulf Coast to encourage churches to rebuild using green techniques. Cassandra admitted that the up-front costs have been the primary deterrent to rebuilding green as churches resurrect their sanctuaries. St. John Baptist Church was no exception. A board of seven church members spearheaded the rebuilding and maintained contact via conference calls with the general contractor, architect, and electrical and mechanical engineers. These professionals also encouraged the church leadership to save money over time with green improvements.

With help from the Eco-Justice Program, the church received a $25,000 grant from Enterprise, a foundation that sponsors green projects. The grant enabled the church to spend $20,000 on energy-efficient windows that were double-insulated and cost twice as much as the cheapest windows. The church also purchased a more efficient air-conditioning and heating system and energy-efficient appliances. Prior to the storm, the church's utility bills were $1,000 a month, but those bills have been cut by 50 percent after the energy-efficient upgrades. For June 2008, a hot month in New Orleans, the utility bill was only $400. While these initiatives may seem small, the savings of $500–$600 a month will prove critical for the sustainability of this church in a neighborhood of both resurrection and decay. An investment of $25,000 will save the congregation $6,000 a year, while decreasing their consumption of God's resources on the earth.

Rev. Boutte talked about his own personal journey of faith and hope after Katrina. God must have a sense of humor, he said, since his role as a pastor had included the jobs of contractor, architect, policy advocate, congressional witness, and insurance expert. Given the impacts of climate change, he said, the demands placed on church leaders call for a different kind of training in seminary, a broader education that includes sustainability in the face of natural disasters. The National Council of Churches asked Rev. Boutte to testify before the U.S. House of Representatives Committee on the Budget regarding housing needs in New Orleans and along the Gulf Coast.[7] He saw this statement before Congress as part of his ministry, as a testimony to sustain the environment and, ultimately, the hope of his parishioners.

As he reflected on his own mental health during the rebuilding, he said that he felt as if he had been fired from his job without a pink slip. But one day, as he drove across the state of Texas to perform a funeral service for a parishioner's brother, God spoke to him: "You might not have a church, but you are still a pastor." With a sense of hope, Rev. Boutte gained strength to face this new way of being a pastor—without buildings or books but with a renewed faith in his call to rebuild a spiritual community.

The Integration and Coordination of Environmental Needs into Rebuilding

The media coverage of Hurricane Katrina focused attention on the neighborhoods of the Upper and Lower Ninth Wards, which received overwhelming damage from the storm surge. Located geographically closer to the mouth of the Mississippi River, the Lower Ninth Ward included fewer rebuilt homes and a larger scale of abandonment. Churches, schools, and stores were empty, but every block or two people sat on the porch of a rebuilt home. These families still faced the challenge of procuring basic necessities like food and medicine, since the neighborhood did not have enough residents to attract such commercial businesses as grocery stores and pharmacies.

If It Had Not Been for the Churches, I Don't Know What Would Have Happened   On a steamy July afternoon in the Upper Ninth Ward, about 150 African American boys and girls, from elementary- to middle-school age, were seated on the gym floor of Desire Street Ministries, where a teen counselor prepared them for a swimming outing the next day. During the summer months, Desire Street Ministries provided this day camp for neighborhood youth. A tall man with a quick smile, ebony skin, and glasses, Tronn Moller arrived at the offices of Desire Street Ministries, where his mother, Marcia Peterson, was the director. Among his other work, Tronn served as a consultant to the National Council of Churches for the Special Commission on the Just Rebuilding of New Orleans.

He coauthored a report that quantified the massive recovery response undertaken by eighteen denominations and Christian relief agencies affiliated with the National Council of Churches in the year following Hurricanes Katrina and Rita.[8] The report begins with a statement heard over and over from Katrina survivors: "If it had not been for the churches, I don't know what would have happened." As the media covered stories of miscommunications and mishaps by the government, the faith community responded quickly with food, shelter, volunteers, and pastoral counseling.

More than $160 million was collected by the eighteen reporting denominations of the NCC in the first year after the storm, with $37.1 million dispersed for recovery activities and $100 million pledged for longer-term projects. Denominations sent teams of volunteers, food, clothing, and supplies for gutting houses, and 50 percent of the denominations and agencies made two- to five-year commitments to repair and rebuild more than 3,100 homes along the Gulf Coast. As concrete examples of this ministry, more than 10,000 homes were gutted and 2,363 repaired, with 1.5 million volunteer hours documented.[9]

The reporting denominations of the NCC include the African Methodist Episcopal Church, the American Baptist Churches USA, the Friends United Meeting, and ecumenical bodies such as Church World Service and the Reformed Church World Service. While the entire report focuses on the just rebuilding of the Gulf Coast, specific examples emphasize environmental concerns. For example, the Jericho Road Housing Initiative, a collaboration of the Episcopal Church, the United Methodist Church, and the United Methodist Committee on Relief, has integrated energy efficiency and green building into the construction of homes in the Central City area near downtown.

What's the New Gumbo That Will Come Out of This? A community organizer, Tronn Moller grew up in New Orleans and led capacity-building efforts for faith-based groups for years. After Katrina, he received funding from the Christian Reformed World Service to partner with faith-based organizations to help them develop their relief efforts and to target justice issues in local communities. At the same time, the National Council of Churches was looking for someone to be its "eyes and ears on the ground" to address eco-justice issues in the rebuilding of the Gulf Coast.

One of the first projects Tronn initiated was capacity building for Churches Supporting Churches, the group headed by Rev. Boutte. From this work, Tronn developed personal relationships with the participating pastors as they thought through the rebuilding process together. He connected pastors with available resources, making calls when, for example, he learned that World Vision had a supply truck coming into town.

Given the limited resources, integrating environmentalism into the rebuilding was often a challenge. Many pastors could not prioritize energy efficiency over short-term costs or available materials. "Cassandra [Carmichael] and Cory Sparks held meetings to promote energy-efficient supplies for pastors, but ultimately, the pastors had to take what they could get," Tronn said. He also helped to organize a listening tour for faith leaders from across the country to bear witness to the environmental issues related to the Katrina disaster, such as mitigating toxins in the soil.[10] To prioritize the environment in rebuilding after natural disasters, he stressed the importance of coordination between denominations. "I think if we could have talked to the disaster response groups of each denomination on a national level to ensure they integrated energy efficiency and the environment into rebuilding, we could have made a more conscious and integrated effort," he said.

Tronn's work with churches after Katrina redefined his relationship to God, forcing him to ask how we can work together to make "thy kingdom come." When he reflected on justice and the Gulf Coast, he posed the question: "What's the new gumbo that will come out of this?" The new gumbo along the Gulf Coast included the mix of Latino, African American, and white residents rebuilding sustainable communities in place and spirit.

Hauling Garbage and Rebuilding Churches on Desire Street   With an easy smile like her son's, Marcia Peterson seemed like the mother of Desire Street Ministries, a Christian agency that advocated for environmental justice, provided education through a boarding school, and nurtured local students through its summer camp program. The website for Desire Street Ministries shows pictures of local kids and videos of the executive director, former football star Danny Wuerffel, who raises funds from his base in Florida. To many, environmental priorities reflect extras like green spaces and organic produce beyond survival needs. But to the residents of Desire Street after Katrina, environmental concerns were as basic as trash removal from the streets.

"We are here to be a voice for equity and justice for how the neighborhoods will be rebuilt," Marcia said. "Last summer, the trash was not getting hauled away, and we had rats as big as cats and dogs." Marcia became "best friends" with the woman who answered the phone at the sanitation department. She would go online to find the name of the owner of the lot and then call 311 to report the trash and request a trash pickup, as if she were the owner. The switchboard operator went along with her requests.

Volunteers and staff at Desire Street Ministries worked to rebuild houses amid a patchwork quilt of abandonment, where some houses were literally falling on top of others. Desire Street Ministries houses 100–150 volunteers from churches each week, with as many as 195 at peak times, such as summer and spring breaks. She expressed strong feelings about the role of churches in transforming the environment of New Orleans. "It would be a total disaster without the churches," she said. From Marcia's perspective, volunteers, mostly from churches, coordinated all the cleanup in the Ninth Ward. But she worried that the plan was to abandon the Ninth Ward and let developers come in to reclaim the property.

Marcia conveyed a vision for the future of New Orleans that draws on her faith. "Without my faith, I don't know how I could face the reality of people still living in FEMA trailers," she said. Marcia believes that the government is waiting for people to die, so that it can take the land. "But I believe that God has wiped the slate clean so people of faith can rebuild in a way God wanted communities to be built."

Rebuilding churches like St. Roch Community Church with energy-efficient techniques was another priority of Desire Street Ministries. The funding for the church's energy-efficient features, such as geothermal heating and cooling systems, came from private donations. Architects from Tulane University, working pro bono, have collaborated on the rebuilding project, and volunteers from Desire Street Ministries poured concrete at the church. The church stood directly across the street from the St. Roch Cemetery, with its white stone sculpture of the Virgin Mary and the raised tombs typical of New Orleans cemeteries. The painted messages on the houses throughout the Ninth Ward were reminders of the hurricane, like this permanent tattoo on a home: "One dog dead. Gave water."

As Marcia said, "How do we deal with natural disasters on a personal level, and how will the church continue to respond? We are now living in a world where natural disasters are the norm." As a joke, Marcia gave each of her family members a gag emergency evacuation kit the Christmas after Katrina. When describing this gift, which included a medical kit, water bottles, and blank documents for financial records, she got tears in her eyes from laughter, but the tears also reflected poignant memories for her.

The Power of Partnerships: Churches Testing for
Toxic Soils

Sometimes, natural disasters push congregations beyond their own sanctuaries. In the case of Carrollton and Parker United Methodist Church, the church became a disaster response center, a site for self-sufficient volunteers to gather and work after Katrina. Over a period of two years, the congregation hosted 3,000 volunteers, providing such amenities as a shower room, storage space for tools, and pastor team leaders to work on rebuilding churches. The church served as command central for as many as eighty volunteers at a time who camped, cooked, and gutted and rebuilt churches with a focus on sustainability.[11]

"We are making a theological stand on the environment," said the Reverend Cory Sparks. "It's not extra. This is at the core of who we are as people of Christ." Rev. Sparks was in his second year of ministry at Carrollton and Parker United Methodist Church when Katrina struck. Since his church did not flood, he organized a meeting in the parsonage to create a plan called Operation New Creation with a focus on immediate assistance. The dust masks the volunteers were using did not provide adequate protection from the high levels of mold, so his group sought assistance on this technical issue from the Louisiana Environmental Action Network (LEAN).

With so many volunteers operating from the church, Rev. Sparks also saw the need to assess the toxicity of the soil where they were working. There had been apocalyptic findings about the toxins released during the hurricane and then found in the soil in communities like Chalmette, Louisiana, and Moss Point, Mississippi. "I was worried about my two-year-old daughter, who has asthma, given the air quality and the soils," Rev. Sparks said. To cover the costs of the testing, Marylee Orr, executive director of LEAN, acquired a donation, and the United Methodist Church gave permission to test the soils of churches in flooded areas, giving access to a broad geographic range of soils. The results showed that heavy metals were the biggest problem, but they were within the range reported as acceptable by the EPA.

For churches seeking to integrate the environment into their work, Rev. Sparks advised seeking partnerships with experts. "Reach out to others, both within and outside the church, who know how to do the work," he said. Within the church, for example, a member who was an architect played a large role in the rebuilding initiatives. And outside the church, Rev. Sparks looked for help from people of faith within the secular environmental movement. The opportunity to blend faith and vocation can be a welcome first for many people working in the environmental field.

Long-Term Economic Gains Promote
Sustainable Communities

Rev. Sparks' church had three levels of response to Katrina: immediate assistance, disaster teams for cleaning and gutting, and a longer-term focus on the environment for rebuilding. "As ministers, we gathered people together and said that we were going to demonstrate the viability of our communities," he said. That focus on energy efficiency and sustainability would be key to rebuilding sustainable faith communities. He reached out to developers and architects, who helped to facilitate planning sessions and charrettes to focus on sustainability, green spaces, and the environment in rebuilding.

Applying the Financial Bottom Line   Churches can recoup much of their initial investments in energy efficiency in three years, Rev. Sparks maintained.[12] Within the church, he advised recognizing the decision makers, because greening has to become part of the normal operations of the church, rather than an add-on like an Earth Day event. Seek out church trustees who will understand the cost savings from energy efficiency, such as anyone who has worked in construction, engineering, or building, he recommended. "We ask these questions in business—how to save money in the long term—but why not the church?" Rev. Sparks said. These questions have to go beyond the "green team" of the church to hit the bottom line of church budgets. When he meets resistance to environmental issues within churches, he finds people from the business community who see the financial sense of sustainability. "You trot out this man or woman in a suit who says green makes financial sense, and people in a church listen," he said. "It is ultimately a theological issue of how you steward God's resources."

Through his organization, Sustainable Churches for South Louisiana, Rev. Sparks recruited AmeriCorps volunteers to provide some of the labor for the sustainable rebuilding of churches. The volunteers conducted training sessions on energy efficiency in churches and have established professional contacts for energy-efficiency audits for churches. They also provided resources for worship and devotion focused on the environment. Churches that have implemented recommendations from the energy audits have saved an average of $2,000 a year through simple changes such as caulking, replacing old appliances, and installing fluorescent lightbulbs.[13] On a broader level, the organization has convened diverse denominations around the table at the Louisiana Interchurch Conference, a gathering of Catholic, Episcopalian, Baptist, and United Methodist clergy, to brainstorm regional solutions to energy conservation among congregations.

In his own church, Rev. Sparks said he did not set aside just one Sunday to focus on creation care as a sideline; he tried to integrate it throughout the year, with numerous outdoor services, presentations, and a teaching ministry that draws from biblical texts to equate faithfulness to God with stewardship. "This is not something new added to the Bible," he emphasized. "We are not doing this because it is trendy, but because it's a part of the gospel." His advice to pastors was to frame stewardship as love for God's creation, a message that resonated with folks who read *Sojourners* and with parishioners who were skeptical of social justice movements.

Recreating Neighborhoods in Central City Downtown New Orleans, with its tall buildings, offices, and restaurants, seemed like a different world from the Ninth Ward. St. Charles Avenue in the Garden District boasted palatial homes and landscaped lawns, a stark contrast to FEMA trailers. In this neighborhood, the office of the Episcopal Diocese of Louisiana sat next to Christ Church Cathedral and the Office of Disaster Response, home of the Jericho Road Housing Initiative.[14] A close friend had described Bishop Charles Jenkins as "a good old boy who had been transformed by the hurricane." Jenkins, a robust man in his late fifties, wore a purple clerical shirt and dark slacks and the polite expression of someone who saw a lot of people every day.

In the diocesan office, the bishop explained that 70 percent of housing in New Orleans was still uninhabitable. The diocese had focused its rebuilding efforts in Central City, due to its proximity to downtown and jobs. In the Central City area, only two blocks from the Garden District, the Jericho Road Housing Initiative had purchased forty-nine lots that had been abandoned and had integrated green trends into affordable home building, including Energy Star-rated appliances and the type of insulation used. He recalled a study by the Kaiser Family Foundation that found that 98 percent of the survivors interviewed at the Houston Astrodome said their faith in God was what enabled them to survive.

As he talked, Bishop Jenkins's face became animated, and he grabbed his keys and wallet to give me a personal tour of the rebuilding project. Driving his SUV a few blocks from the diocesan office, he talked about the theological reasons for working in Central City. "This ministry is based on the dignity of every human being and the New Testament virtue of charity in the strict theological sense," he said. He emphasized the connection between the rebuilding work, our baptismal covenant, and the dignity of all people. The Jericho Road project was building homes that use green materials so that people could become homeowners and, ultimately, save money on utilities.

To promote transparency, religious leaders in this neighborhood formed the Central City Pastors to coordinate the denominations in the area. "We're partnering with an evangelical group from Kentucky," the bishop said. "The nature of the ecumenical alliances in this work has been inspiring—Episcopalians, evangelicals, and a soul-food restaurant." Just around the corner, the next stop was a Brownfield site owned by the city of New Orleans. Less than a mile from the grandeur of St. Charles Avenue was a world of abandoned houses interspersed with some rebuilt homes (fig. 4.2). A group of volunteers worked on a small, colorful house with a sign that announced the Jericho Road Housing Initiative.

The bishop admitted to feeling bitter about "predators" in New Orleans, who were taking advantage of "people who are desperate" by offering a gospel of prosperity. When he slowed the car on Sixth Street to speak to volunteers, Bishop Jenkins pointed out the group of four rebuilt houses in the same block, rather than one house in the

Figure 4.2   Churches and faith organizations took the lead in the recovery efforts after Katrina by rebuilding homes, often in the midst of abandoned lots. Photo by the author.

middle of decay. The houses were pastel-colored bungalows that fit into the architectural style of New Orleans. "We are bunching the houses together to create a neighborhood feel," he said. "And we're now training local kids in the construction." The project has built and sold twenty houses in this program, which lends people the down payment and forgives the loan if the occupants stay in the house for five years. Most of the people buying homes have been former Central City residents.[15]

This natural disaster and the rebuilding had a deep impact on this bishop, who could not have imagined his ministry in a post-Katrina world.[16] "I have written about the night of my breaking and despair," he said. "The idea I had about being a bishop was washed away with Katrina. As I sat there in Baton Rouge and heard the convoy on the interstate, I knew that if I was going to be a bishop, I needed grace to be something different." Bishop Jenkins recognized that there are children in the Ninth Ward who have not been past Canal Street. He described New Orleans as America's opportunity to address classism, racism, intentionally bad education, and intentionally bad economic policies. "Mercy means giving someone more than they deserve," he said. Months after this tour with me, Bishop Jenkins announced his intention to step down from his position, in part because of the post-traumatic stress he has suffered after Katrina.

Responding to Natural Disaster and Rebuilding
as a Ministry: Lessons Learned

Churches will continue to heed the biblical call to respond to people and places in need. This Christian response becomes a prayer in communion, as people of faith pull their emotional and financial resources together to help neighbor and stranger alike. In turn, spiritual communities are transformed. And ultimately, responding to disaster is about a long-term presence in a community, not just about relief. Bishop Jenkins kept repeating this point as we drove around Central City. "We are not just about disaster relief," he said, "but also about rebuilding and development, which is our long-term work." His words reflect the message of Cassandra Carmichael that climate change is happening to God's people, to us.

What is the cumulative impact of the stories from these natural saints, who were transformed by their own ministries in community? The stories encountered along the Gulf Coast reveal the following best practices to guide churches as we respond to natural disasters and integrate environmental values into that response.

Emphasize the hope that comes from faith communities as we face the rebuilding of communities.

The religious community responds to natural disasters out of a biblical call for mercy but also because of a theological message of hope. The Gulf Coast stories reflect a metaphor used by Katy Hinman of the religious environmental group Georgia Interfaith Power & Light. She said that the science of climate change and the environmental crisis is the wake-up call. But faith in God provides the hope that gets us out of bed to do something about it. Faith gives us the hope, joy, and possibility of triumph to "let not our hearts be troubled" but to move forward with action. And ultimately, this hope is what the religious community can offer that the secular environmental groups have not been able to provide.

Integrate and coordinate sustainability into disaster relief and rebuilding.

Without sustainability as a priority in disaster relief, we may end up rebuilding in ways that fail to serve the long-term interests of communities. A focus on sustainability can encourage churches involved in disaster relief to communicate about materials, resources, and rebuilding plans that promote just environments. As Christians, when we approach relief and rebuilding as a ministry, we must begin to consider our impact on social, economic, and ecological systems. Too often, denominations work without coordinating immediate assistance, particularly when the need is high. Coordination and communication can help to ensure that priority is given to long-term economic and environmental gains in materials and other resources.

Partner with secular environmentalists who are people of faith.

Many staff in environmental agencies and nonprofits include people of faith eager to connect their faith with their vocation. Most churches and communities have potential partnerships with environmental organizations that could provide both expertise and legitimacy to religious environmental work. Consider using the natural resources of the church to further environmental causes, such as the testing for toxins that was done in the soils of church grounds in southern Louisiana.

Emphasize the long-term economic gains from investing in green building and energy efficiency and recruit church members who understand the economic bottom line.

Churches have a long history of financial stewardship and tithing to sustain both institutions and ministries. Church members who are integrating the environment into disaster relief or any other ministry should target those in the church who deal with business and finance and stress long-term gains through short-term investments. In the end, we must showcase the economic gains from energy efficiency and green building for the viability of our spiritual communities and our environments.

On Reflection

As a young person in the church, I often thought about disaster relief in terms of the coins I put in a little blue UNICEF cardboard box and gave to the ushers one Sunday each year. I had a vague and inaccurate mental image of God's children "over there" who needed help because of earthquakes, hurricanes, and flooding. Yet I grew up in a coastal area prone to hurricanes, where my dad had a special radio that broadcast only the weather. We even had a cross-stitched hurricane-tracking chart hanging on the bright yellow wall of our kitchen. The connection between local disasters and injustice hit me as a teenager when I experienced hurricanes in Fairhope, Alabama. I realized that community members living in mobile homes were the first to lose their homes to hurricanes. The stories I found along the Gulf Coast during my visit showed me that disaster response is about being in community with others and enhancing the sustainability of both people and place.

The morning before my interviews at Desire Street Ministries, I spent several hours on a rental bike riding around the neighborhoods of the Upper and Lower Ninth wards. Seeing the patchwork quilt of rebuilt homes next to blighted structures felt less intrusive from a bicycle than from a car. Driving in a car around the neighborhoods by St. John Baptist Church, I felt like a disaster junkie, separated from the people sitting on the front porches. A bike allowed me to say hello to people in the neighborhoods, navigate the one-way streets and the large potholes found at every turn, and conduct interviews without using fossil fuels.

As I biked around New Orleans, I felt the surreal contrast between the tourist districts and the continuing devastation—four years after Katrina—of the Lower Ninth Ward. The French Quarter looked unscathed in comparison to much of the city. Outside, it was ninety-five degrees, yet tourists sat on the porch of the Café du Monde drinking hot coffee and eating beignets covered in powdered sugar. Step dancers performed before crowds on the sidewalks, and restaurants boiled vats of shrimp and crayfish spiced with the distinctive smell of crab boil. These classic New Orleans streetscapes felt like an orchestrated movie scene in the face of the kudzu overtaking the crumbling homes in other areas of the city.

Despite the hope shown by the people I encountered, I wondered how they managed to keep that faith in the face of natural disaster. I experienced the same disbelief after the earthquake in Haiti, when all I could do to help was to donate a small amount of money and pray. In Louisiana, Rev. Sparks, who served at Carrollton and Parker United Methodist Church, said that the storm "revolutionized" his thinking about ministry. The people of faith I met in New Orleans described personal transformations through their encounters with each other as they regained and rebuilt their communities. I witnessed again faith in the unseen. Despite our best efforts to shape the environment around us, a natural disaster turns our sense of control upside down. What we *can* control is how we respond so as to mitigate the impacts and rebuild with God's world at the forefront of our efforts. Mercy means giving both people and places more than they deserve.

5

Promoting Justice

Environmental Justice, Toxic Tours, and GreenFaith

*He loves righteousness and justice; the earth is full of the
steadfast love of the Lord.*

—Psalm 33:5 (NRSV)

*Justice is a foundation of all religions. If the religious
environmental movement focuses too much on energy
conservation in our houses of worship, we will miss a big
opportunity to affect change on a societal level. We've got
to reclaim justice as a primary focus of the religious
environmental movement.*

—Rev. Fletcher Harper, executive director,
GreenFaith

With his narrow glasses, short gray and black hair, and soft voice,
Ted Carrington stood before a group of twenty religious leaders who
had gathered in the wooden pews of the Church of our Savior to
learn about the environmental justice work of GreenFaith, a religious environmental organization based in New Jersey. A quaint
Episcopal church in Secaucus, New Jersey, this small, white-paneled
church with a red door was ordered from Sears, Roebuck as a prefabricated house of worship. The director of environmental justice
for GreenFaith, Ted described his experience conducting air monitoring with high-school students using hand-held monitors. The

students from nearby high schools watched the measurements of fine and ultra-fine particulates increase as a bus or truck drove past. "We were at one intersection—it was the perfect storm—where the New Jersey Turnpike crosses Route 1," he said. "We were getting our measurements, and all the kids started having asthma attacks." He and the students had to leave the monitoring site because the air was so unhealthy.

New Jersey has the third-highest diesel emissions rate in the United States, following New York and California, and diesel emissions are the leading cause of asthma attacks in children. Indeed, reducing the amount of diesel emissions by 20 percent could prevent about 900 deaths each year in New Jersey.[1] As part of a diesel emissions campaign, New Jersey's environmental justice community used air monitoring as an outreach strategy with students in the historically polluted cities of Camden, Newark, and Trenton.[2]

GreenFaith took additional steps, providing resources for congregations to address diesel emissions with a sample letter to the governor, a bulletin insert, and a fact sheet on the health implications of diesel emissions.[3] Houses of worship sent more than 1,500 letters, advocating that the governor require companies with state contracts to retrofit diesel on-road vehicles and construction equipment. Churches can confront environmental inequities by promoting justice through voices in the pulpit, action on the pavement, and advocacy for just environmental policies. This chapter details how people of faith in New Jersey and New York are reclaiming a ministry of justice with a focus on the environment.

"All communities, it turns out, are not created equal. Some get dumped on more than others," writes religious leader Larry Rasmussen.[4] The environmental justice movement addresses the inequitable environmental burden placed on people of color and the poor and attempts to overcome the power structures that have gotten in the way of environmental reforms.[5] Religious leaders working for environmental justice believe that "the environment" includes "where we live, work, play, and pray."[6] With a history of involvement in social justice movements, congregations are transforming this theological mandate to work toward environmental justice in local communities.

Indeed, faith communities helped to define environmental justice as a national movement in the United States. In 1987, churches were involved in what would become the defining case study for environmental justice. In Warren County, North Carolina, a PCB (polychlorinated biphenyl) landfill was sited in an African American community, which asked the United Church of Christ Commission for Racial Justice to protest the decision. Five hundred people were arrested during the protest.[7] Incidents similar to the Warren County siting prompted Ben Chavis, executive director of the United Church of Christ Commission for Racial Justice, to commission a national study to look at the connection between race and the location of toxic waste sites.

Chavis coined the phrase *environmental racism* in the subsequent 1987 report, *Toxic Waste and Race in the US*. This report documented the intentional placement of toxic incinerators, landfills, and other polluting industries in communities of color and the poor.[8] A year before the Warren County incident, in 1986, Cora Tucker, a member of Crystal Hills Baptist Church, organized the local black community through its churches to fight a nuclear waste dump in Halifax County, Virginia. "The real organized groups in the U.S. are churches," Tucker said.[9]

In partnership with both congregations and secular environmental groups, GreenFaith addresses its mission to "inspire, educate, and mobilize people from diverse spiritual backgrounds to rediscover their relationship with the sacred in nature and to restore the earth for future generations."[10] GreenFaith's focus on justice has elevated the relevance of religious communities in the protection of people and places exposed to environmental injustices. This chapter highlights the work of GreenFaith and its partnerships with the West Harlem Environmental Action Coalition (WE ACT) and St. Mary's Episcopal Church in Harlem. This chapter also introduces Cecil Corbin-Marks, an activist who works to bring people of faith into the environmental justice movement, and the Reverend Fletcher Harper, who believes deeply that religious groups are called to advocate for environmental justice. The lessons learned from these stories include the impact of outreach strategies like toxic tours; the power of prayer, ritual, and hope; the potential of partnerships; the position of the church as a first responder to environmental injustice; and the importance of justice as a religious framework.

Toxic Tours: Travel with a Purpose Grounded in Faith

On a small patch of grass near the entrance to the Newark incinerator, a group of twenty priests, nuns, rabbis, and lay leaders stood in a circle. A multicolored metal building, larger than several football fields, the incinerator was adjacent to the New Jersey Turnpike where the students experienced asthma attacks during the air monitoring. As the religious leaders watched, gray garbage trucks barreled past the metal fence surrounding the incinerator. Each had a New York license plate, an indication of the dumping ground that Newark had become: 50 percent of the garbage that came to the Newark incinerator was from New York City. In the 1980s, fierce political pressure from suburban communities resulted in the construction of only two incinerators in the region, one in Newark and one in Camden, New Jersey.

A new brand of tourism, toxic tours aim to increase awareness of the inequitable distribution of pollutants in communities and the work of grassroots groups advocating for justice. For GreenFaith, the overall goal of these tours is to inspire people of faith to take concrete steps to mitigate these environmental injustices. This group of religious leaders—GreenFaith fellows—had gathered for a four-day retreat on environmental justice as part of a GreenFaith initiative to build religious environmental leadership. The incinerator was the first stop on a tour of toxic sites in the Newark area. As garbage trucks whizzed past on this toxic tour, the GreenFaith fellows listened to the story of two Catholic nuns who taught at Resurrection School in Jersey City, a site downwind from the incinerator and subject to its harmful emissions.

The nuns' location downwind of the incinerator gave Green-Faith standing to sue under the Clean Air Act. Their belief that "all God's children breathe the same air" gave weight to the lawsuit, which protested emissions from the Newark incinerator that impacted the health of the parochial school's students. "People of faith have a powerful voice when they speak," said Rev. Fletcher Harper, executive director of GreenFaith and an Episcopal priest. In such lawsuits, GreenFaith relies on environmental law clinics from universities and on regional and national environmental law firms.

In partnership with the neighboring Ironbound Community Corporation, GreenFaith sent a letter of intent to sue due to the mercury emissions from the incinerator. The Ironbound community is home to two low-income federal housing complexes and is located only a half mile from the incinerator, which is adjacent to two of the community's poorest tracts, home to 8,000 people. The incinerator emits 200 pounds of mercury each year into the air.[11] In the intent to sue, the Ironbound Community Corporation and GreenFaith asked for increased inspections, decreased pollution, and $600,000 for the Ironbound community for green initiatives such as open space for community parks. "Sometimes the threat of legal action truly does get the attention of these powerful polluting groups," said Rev. Harper. He explained that the mercury and particulates in the air both had significant impacts on the health of residents, with a large resulting cost to the community.

A yellow-and-black school bus, number thirty-four, provided transportation on this toxic tour. Participants on the tour rode in the same type of government-owned vehicle that produces diesel emissions in the transportation of children to school (fig. 5.1). After a five-minute drive on highways and small industrial roads, the bus approached the second stop on the toxic tour, the Diamond Shamrock Chemicals Company. A chain-link fence surrounded this Superfund site, which contained one of the world's largest concentrations of dioxin. Behind the group, spray paint on a green wall spelled "child molester." Circular barbed wire bordered the top of the fence, catching random plastic bags that resembled plastic birds fluttering in the sky.

For more than a hundred years, different manufacturing companies had used this property, and in the mid-1940s the industry shifted to production of DDT and phenoxy herbicides, the Agent Orange used in the Vietnam War. In 1983, sampling at the site revealed significant levels

Figure 5.1 GreenFaith's toxic tour showed participants the connections between faith and environmental justice by traveling on a school bus to sites such as the Newark incinerator. Photo by the author.

of contamination from dioxin. The then-owner of the property, Occidental Chemicals Company, was required to remediate the site, which involved putting a cement cap over barrels of dioxin stored adjacent to the Passaic River. Remediation of the river will take decades and cost hundreds of millions of dollars. Seventeen miles of the river have been declared a Superfund site under the Superfund law, which was created to protect communities from contaminated toxic waste sites that have been abandoned.

Faced with this story and these statistics, a woman in our group of GreenFaith fellows raised her hand and said, "I feel like we need some space to respond through prayer to what we have seen." Everyone— rabbis, priests, pastors, nuns, and laypeople—nodded in unison; all needed a spiritual response to these injustices. Rev. Harper reminded us, "This is where you have to claim your religious identity as the reason why poor communities should not have to live near these toxic sites." The faith leaders agreed to make time for individual and collective prayer at the end of the tour.

The school bus continued only a mile or two before stopping at a recreation center in the Newark neighborhood of Ironbound, where one of every four residents lives in poverty in this community bordered by an airport, a highway, a rail line, and the Passaic River.[12] Ted explained that, due to the lead content in the soil, the recreation center was built on cement pillars, ten feet above the contaminated ground. A football field next to the recreation center was surrounded by a locked chain-link fence with a sign that read "Attention: Athletic fields temporarily closed by order of City of Newark Department of Health and Human Services." The contaminated ground had been dug up, as if children had been let loose with shovels on the field. Due to dangerously high levels of lead in the soil, the athletic field had been closed since 1987.

As Ted spoke, planes flew overhead, and traffic roared past. Every minute or two, another screaming plane departed or landed at Newark Airport, while the garbage and dump trucks revved their engines and drove through water in the potholes. Ted paused, realizing the impossibility of being heard above the surrounding noise. One member of the group shouted, "We have no idea what the stress level is to people who live here." Just down the road, a class of toddlers played tag with their teachers in the concrete parking lot.

The purpose of these toxic tours is not to send people into the dumps of despair after seeing the literal dumping grounds of our own waste. Rather, these tours introduce participants to community members and organizations that partner with GreenFaith to make a difference. One such grassroots group, the Ironbound Community Corporation, founded in 1969, provides facilities such as a daycare center, and services, including community organizing, for the 50,000 people in this neighborhood, which comprises fifty-four different ethnic groups.[13] According to the Ironbound Community Corporation website, the Ironbound zip code 07105 is the worst pollution emitter in New Jersey, though not through any fault of its residents, most of whom fall into one or more of the following categories: low-income, non-English-speaking, recent immigrants, and people of color.

The Ironbound Community Corporation has conducted extensive community organizing to improve the quality of life and the environmental health of its residents, such as leading efforts for a scenic greenbelt along the riverfront. In facilitating these tours for environmental justice, GreenFaith works with Ironbound community members who identify the sites and then initiate the tour at Newark Baptist Church. GreenFaith always provides resources for the participants to take action in their congregations on these environmental justice issues. According to Rev. Harper, groups from congregations are often the most effective participants in the tours, as they can work together afterward from their houses of worship.

Pabst Blue Ribbon and the Power of Prayer, Ritual, and Hope

The last stop of the tour featured an old Pabst Blue Ribbon brewery site, 300,000 square feet of lead-painted surfaces in a neighborhood of houses, restaurants, and a cemetery. When construction workers began tearing down the site, they discovered lead and asbestos but had no plans to mitigate impacts to themselves or the nearby residents. A Baptist pastor, Jethro Jones, started organizing the community to put safeguards in place. At the time, there was no fencing around the site, and people were salvaging items, including contaminated scrap metal. Thanks to the efforts of Pastor Jones, the crews are now using safer methods for demolition.

The group of GreenFaith fellows stood in a circle, observing the demolition zone that included the shell of a tall concrete building, which looked as if it had been hit by bombs. Surrounded by single-family homes painted in greens and browns, the brewery site was located in the middle of the neighborhood, much as a park would center a community. In this case, however, piles of rock and dirt and pieces of metal filled the fenced space. John Deere bulldozers and an orange wrecking ball penetrated the building's shell while men in hard hats coordinated the demolition.

In the circle, someone reminded the group of the call to prayer, as the enormity of the problems felt larger than intellectual analysis could handle. Standing by the demolished brewery, twenty people of faith prayed in a public circle, led by Rabbi Larry Troster of Green-Faith (fig. 5.2). Two community residents poked their heads out of their apartment doors to stare at this eclectic religious group with yarmulkes, clerical collars, and crucifixes, a group of faith leaders who prayed as a vocation, who responded to the mysteries of birth and death and life through prayer.

With eyes closed, the group of "tourists" called on God to give healing to the people and places affected by toxic injustices. They prayed for strength in the fight for justice, to use themselves as instruments of healing, hope, peace, and redemption. Somehow, strength came from the collective faith of those who held hands in this circle of prayer and ritual. In closing, Kathleen, a nun and Celtic musician, raised her soprano voice to sing for God to bless and give health "for the cities we are building." Everyone squeezed hands and embraced each other, trusting that they would work in their home

Figure 5.2   Religious environmental leaders offered prayers of healing and reconciliation at sites of environmental injustice in New Jersey. Photo by the author.

communities to fight similar battles as those in the Ironbound Community Corporation.

After returning to the church, the group sat in a circle to pray, hold silence, and then share impressions from the tour. Frank, an Episcopal priest from Cincinnati, confessed, "At the waste incinerator, I didn't want to take a breath because I knew what was in the air. I honestly just wanted to get out of there." Nelson, a Lutheran who works with Colorado Interfaith Power & Light, spoke of the spiritual crisis he experienced on the tour. "When we stood by the football fields, I had the feeling of being assaulted with the planes flying by, the trucks driving by, and all the noise," he said. "I just kept thinking of the psychic toll that would take on me. I would die by some violent means before the particulates in the air killed me."

While some felt overwhelmed, others drew strength from learning how faith communities are responding to these environmental inequities. Before going to seminary, Martha, an Episcopal priest, worked as the commissioner of the Maine Department of Environmental Protection. "I have been to sites just like the ones we saw today, but I saw them from the perspective of a regulator," she said. "And today, I was coming in a community of faith. It was a completely different and empowering experience." Despite the diverse impacts of the tour, everyone agreed they were affected in some profound way as they bore witness to the collective environmental sins of our society.

After the tour, Rev. Harper reminded the faith leaders of the potential power of religion in the environmental movement. "A primary communication strategy of the environmental movement has been apocalyptic, which scares people and turns them off," he said. In contrast, when Rev. Harper addresses a group, he always starts with a story about people's connection with the natural world. One of the reasons that religion is getting traction in the environmental movement is because religion is about *hope*. "As religious people, we have a remarkable advantage of having networks of people capable of affecting change through planning and hope," he said. "The environmental community sees us as having a great advantage in this work." Religion can help us to make a prayerful response to the environments around us, but religion is also *in* the world. It's about work. Hope is the difference that religion offers to the environmental movement.

In speaking of hope, Rabbi Troster clarified the role of ritual in giving people hope to confront environmental realities. He explained that his devotion to the rituals of his faith and to his family prevented him from despair. "Some of the suffering from the state of our environment can be dealt with through liturgy and ritual in community," he said. "How do we ritualize the fear, anger, and despair, so we can renew ourselves to confront the world? This is the role of religion." As he prayed with sacred objects each day, he modeled that power of ritual, which gave him traction as he worked with interfaith audiences to promote justice.

Partnerships with Secular Environmental Groups
for Justice

The impact of churches on justice becomes greater in partnership with other environmental organizations that work in local communities. To leverage this power, GreenFaith partners with environmental justice organizations in urban areas, such as WE ACT, the West Harlem Environmental Action Coalition. As he talked to the GreenFaith fellows, the deputy director of WE ACT, Cecil Corbin-Marks, was dressed in a perfectly tailored linen suit. Cecil defined environmental racism as the inequitable distribution of environmental benefits and burdens to communities and the structural systems that deliver them. The group of fellows passed around a photocopied manual provided by Lois Gibbs's Center for Health, Environment & Justice titled *Political Difficulties Facing Waste-to-Energy Conversion Plant Siting.*[14] Published by California Waste Management, the manual outlines strategies for choosing locations for incinerators and advises targeting poor rural communities and avoiding wealthy suburban neighborhoods.

The executive director of WE ACT, Peggy Shepherd, discussed the early days of the organization, and her words reflected the potential power of churches in the environmental movement. Peggy's work in environmental justice has been featured in many publications, including *Newsweek* and the *Christian Science Monitor.* She described the founding of WE ACT in 1988, after the United Church of Christ published the report *Toxic Waste and Race in the US.* Soon after, in 1991, seventeen principles of environmental justice were developed at the First National People of Color Environmental Justice Summit, a historic multiethnic gathering.[15] Early organizing efforts targeted the EPA and its lack of focus on environmental justice. "In 1992, we found a memo from inside the EPA that said the environmental justice groups shouldn't merge with faith groups—the partnership would be just too powerful," Peggy said. She noted that WE ACT began through collaborations with churches, such as St. Mary's Episcopal Church in West Harlem.

On April 30, 2008, WE ACT brought together fifty leaders of churches, mosques, and synagogues from northern Manhattan to build a religious network for training and collaborative work, the Faith Leaders for Environmental Justice network. This 7.25-square-mile area of Harlem and Washington Heights is home to 650,000 residents and contains six of the seven diesel bus depots in Manhattan, as well as two sewage-treatment plants. The successes of WE ACT have included lobbying for legislation to protect families from lead poisoning; suing the Metropolitan Transportation Authority for building diesel depots; training 200 people as environmental health advocates; training community members in land-use decision making; and advocating for the Harlem River Park, which opened in the summer of 2008.

The Church as a First Responder for Justice

The WE ACT office building was located next to the historic Apollo Theater and across from an Old Navy clothing store in West Harlem. This neighborhood alone was home to 200 churches, from small storefronts to megachurches. When I visited, the office featured posters of direct actions and media clippings of campaign victories. In his twenties, Charles Callaway had worked with WE ACT for a year and was responsible for organizing clergy breakfasts for environmental justice and spearheading campaigns targeting faith leaders. "In the black community, a lot of our members attend church," Charles said. "If we educate the pastors about the issues facing their community, they can make a huge impact." A poster in the hallway of the WE ACT office featured an ad, "Breathe at your own risk," which was placed in city buses during a diesel emissions campaign led by WE ACT in collaboration with churches.

Charles described the Mother Clara Hale Bus Depot campaign, which involved a bus depot located on 125th Street and Lenox Avenue. The Metropolitan Transportation Authority's reconstruction of the depot included removal of asbestos and lead paint, and abatement of the soil. WE ACT helped to organize a task force within the community to act as a watchdog and to ensure that the rebuilding used proper abatement technologies. Two faith communities worked as first responders and partners in this campaign, the Greater Hood AME Church on 146th Street and HCCI, Harlem Congregations for Community Improvement.

As the community organizer for northern Manhattan, Charles involved pastors and churches in other projects, such as a pests and pesticides campaign that included a study on how people dispose of garbage in public housing. Garbage in the neighborhood often attracts rats and other rodents, which infest the buildings, and then the public housing maintenance staff uses strong pesticides to get the rodents out. "We're seeing the health impacts of using these chemicals in an indoor environment, so we're working with churches on this as a part of the Healthy Home campaign," Charles said. Churches have partnered with WE ACT to address environmental justice in both indoor and outdoor environments.

Faith leaders spend much of their time in the critical roles of visiting the homebound, going to the hospital, performing funerals. In doing this important work, however, they often are dealing with the outcomes of environmental injustices, rather than preventing the problems with the help of their churches. Pastors, rabbis, and priests confront their parishioners at the end of a long chain of environmental events: they minister to the sick and make efforts to prevent illnesses such as asthma exacerbated by poor air quality, heart attacks provoked by respiratory disease, and obesity caused by poor-quality foods.

Cassandra Carmichael of the National Council of Churches Eco-Justice Program often speaks about churches working as the "first responder" to climate injustice. When we only minister to the sick, the church is operating as the *last* responder, literally performing last rites on a body that is a victim of environmental degradation. As first responders, churches would organize with communities to advocate for environmental justice since we all breathe the same air in God's world.

Reclaiming Justice as a Religious Framework

Just a few blocks from WE ACT's West Harlem office, St. Mary's Episcopal Church was surrounded by public housing: twenty-two-story buildings named Manhattanville, Grant, and Morningside. A banner hung from the church fence that proclaimed the mission: "St. Mary's Manhattanville is the 'I am not afraid' church, standing up as a community of faith in West Harlem to pursue justice and peace for the poor and oppressed, to pray and care for the sick, lonely, and at risk, and to put into practice the message of the gospel by the power of the Holy Spirit. Do not be afraid. Luke 1:30." St. Mary's exemplified the power of the church to reclaim justice as a ministry focused on the environment, which strengthened the relevance of the congregation in a community facing so many environmental challenges.

On a fall Sunday morning at St. Mary's, church members, both black and white, spent the time before the service catching up with each other in a sanctuary with brightly colored sashes in green, red, and white hanging from the dark wooden rafters. The Reverend Earl Kooperkamp focused on the gospel for the day, Matthew 7:21–27, a passage that speaks of flooding and winds, relevant images in the midst of earthquakes in China, disaster in Myanmar, and Hurricane Katrina. Rev. Kooperkamp spoke directly of the environmental injustices that would come from climate change. He told the congregants that the impacts of climate change would fall hardest on the poorest and reminded us of the U.S. government's lack of response to the victims of Katrina. He brought the point home by noting that the basement below the sanctuary was the lowest point in Manhattan.

Charcoal smoke wafted across the pews from preparations for a cookout after the service. At the barbeque, choir director Sheldon Garland explained to me that he once had sung with the group the Dramatics. "I've been at St. Mary's for twenty years," he said. "I was homeless, but now I have a three-bedroom place and a good job." St. Mary's provided both a sense of place and justice during Sheldon's journey from homelessness to employment.

Rev. Kooperkamp, who was one of the founding board members of WE ACT, attended seminary with Rev. Harper, the executive director of GreenFaith. Piles of letters, postcards, and bills filled Kooperkamp's office, because the church served as the unofficial post office for about 150 people, most of whom were homeless. If sense of place was an environmental construct, then St. Mary's connected people to place through its ad hoc post office. Rev. Kooperkamp recalled working with churches in a long-term battle to shut down the largest medical incinerator on the East Coast, which was located in an area with a high pediatric asthma rate. The incinerator was slated for construction only a few blocks from St. Anne's Church in the South Bronx, where he was the pastor. "It took us seven years, five months, and thirteen days, but we shut it down," he said. Rev. Kooperkamp believes that this focus on justice stands as the essential role of the church in the environmental movement.

The environmental justice work at St. Mary's has included campaigns to close diesel bus depots, like the six in Harlem, which concentrate idling buses in low-income areas. "In our Sunday school classes, thirty percent of the children have asthma," he said. Asthma is exacerbated by diesel particulates, as well as poor indoor air quality, and remains the leading reason that students miss school in urban environments. Rev. Kooperkamp described an Easter Sunday when he planned to preach a sermon about asthma, and before the sermon, one member of the choir had an asthma attack.

The church was working with the administrators of the public housing projects in the neighborhood to promote integrated pest management[16] to improve air quality and reduce asthma, given that 40 percent of the church members live in public housing within a mile of the church.

This ministry of environmental justice can transform religious institutions, whether church members live in public housing, rural neighborhoods, or suburban gated communities. Matthew 22:39 says: "You shall love the Lord your God, with all your heart, and with all your soul, and with all your mind. This is the greatest and first commandment. And a second is like it: 'You shall love your neighbor as yourself'" (NRSV). Indeed, Green-Faith has developed religious principles to guide environmental justice work: "called to protect the earth" principles for advocacy.[17] Available on its website, the principles provide useful guidance when discussing issues of justice in congregations; they focus on the mandates to protect all living things, care for the poor, work for environmental justice, steward the earth, and view the earth as a beloved creation. As Rev. Harper said, "Justice is a foundation of all religions. If the religious environmental movement focuses too much on energy conservation in our houses of worship, we will miss a big opportunity to affect change on a societal level. We've got to reclaim justice as a primary focus of the religious environmental movement."

Promoting Justice as a Ministry: Lessons Learned

My interactions with religious leaders working for environmental justice reveal best practices that can guide us as a communion of saints. By integrating these lessons into their ministries, churches can reclaim justice as a value and enhance their relevance in local environments and in their congregations as well.

Examine environmental justice issues in local communities through outreach strategies like toxic tours.

Many faith organizations are organizing justice tours for congregations, such as climate justice tours that examine the impacts of energy use or toxic tours that highlight sites of environmental injustice. These tours provide education as well as an impetus for action in local churches. Christian education groups, men's and women's groups, youth groups, and green teams provide the perfect existing audiences for these educational tours, which then create opportunities to share and take action with the broader congregation.

Use ritual, prayer, and hope as ways to help Christians respond to the enormity of environmental justice issues.

Christians turn to prayer, liturgy, and sacred texts for answers in confusing times. Each week, people of faith use the power of prayer to respond to issues involving birth and death, and we must call on these familiar strategies in times of environmental uncertainty. Throughout history, religion has given people hope to persevere in the face of looming challenges, including slavery and environmental destruction. Many people have tired of the apocalyptic messages from some mainstream environmental groups, but churches can use a sincere message of hope based on stewardship of God's creation.

Identify and partner with environmental groups focusing on issues of justice.

Most communities or regions include secular environmental groups addressing environmental justice issues, either directly or indirectly. Often, these groups are eager to partner with the organized networks and to engage the theological mandates for justice that churches provide. The book *Blessed Unrest* provides countless examples of grassroots organizations working for environmental and social justice, with an estimate of more than a million such organizations worldwide.[18] Begin small by asking an environmental group to speak to an adult education class. Then, consider ways to build the partnership based on mutual interests.

Position the church as a first responder to environmental injustice.

Faith leaders are called to hospitals, hospices, and funeral homes to pray for healing or to perform last rites, as people fall ill or die due to toxins in our environment. Increasingly, these toxins are affecting not only the poor among us, but all of us. We must position the church as a first responder to address the causes of environmental illness, including particulates in the air and pesticides in our food.

Reclaim justice as a primary religious framework and an integral part of the religious environmental movement.

Justice is a foundation of all religions, and working on environmental justice issues may be one of the central strategies for reclaiming that ministry. This focus on justice provides an accessible entry into environmental action for audiences who may not resonate with typical environmental messages. In the end, Christians believe that we are *all* children of God, which is a central tenet of justice. A focus on justice also addresses institutional power structures in local environments in a way that a focus on mere energy efficiency cannot. While the emphasis on energy efficiency among churches is important, the religious environmental movement must pay attention to issues of equity and access to resources in our communities. Environmental justice broadens our scope and our impact in the environmental movement.

On Reflection

Before entering the GreenFaith fellowship program, I participated in a toxic tour in Roxbury, Massachusetts, outside Boston, with the environmental justice organization called ACE (Alternatives for Community and Environment). I took the walking tour of Roxbury with a group of environmentalists, all passionate, highly educated people, who processed the experience with the language of intellectuals and activists. We spoke about power structures, access to decision making, and inequities. On the GreenFaith toxic tour, I was not prepared to encounter the same types of sites—incinerators, dioxin dumping grounds—with the language of prayer.

As an Episcopalian, I didn't grow up experiencing public prayer, so standing in a prayer circle in broad daylight in the middle of a Newark neighborhood was a new religious experience for me. At the Pabst Brewery site, I stood in a circle with the GreenFaith fellows and closed my eyes as Rabbi Troster led us in prayer. In my initial discomfort, I kept opening my eyes, feeling the real or imagined stares of community members walking the streets. After a few minutes, however, I relaxed into the prayer circle, recognizing the devastation I had felt from seeing the toxic sites and realizing that prayer for justice was the appropriate response. I felt a release from the overwhelming burden of intellectual analysis about these injustices and allowed myself to have an emotional response surrounded by people of faith.

In the words of my own faith, I gave myself over to the prayer. In this circle, I could feel the collective pull of our prayers and song. We created sacred space in the prayerful desire for healing and action. Too often in my life as an environmentalist, I have felt like a closet Christian, pulling out my faith only in safe places, such as church. This religious encounter with environmental injustices in New Jersey made me listen to God calling me to pray for injustices in my home community.

Other GreenFaith fellows had similar responses, as several have organized tours as an outreach strategy in their home communities. Joe Mitchell, a Catholic priest in Kentucky, organized a toxic tour in the Louisville area. In her role with North Carolina Interfaith Power & Light, Jill Rios is working to organize energy justice tours across the state of North Carolina, and my own students conducted preliminary research to identify sites for the tour. In the end, prayer and action are responses to the prejudice and power that create environmental injustices around us. And this ministry of justice allows us to claim our religious identity as a reason for clean and healthy places to live, work, play, and pray.

6

Making a Pilgrimage

Mountaintop Removal, Water, and Wildflowers

On the last day of the festival, the great day, while Jesus was standing there, he cried out, "Let anyone who is thirsty come to me, and let the one who believes in me drink."

—John 7:37 (NRSV)

I have only one thing to say—don't drink the water. Don't drink the water. You can drink it, but it's at your own risk.

—Kevin Pentz, Kentuckians for the Commonwealth

On October 11, 2000, just after midnight, 350 million gallons of coal slurry flooded Martin County, Kentucky, from coal-mine impoundment dams operated by Martin County Coal, a subsidiary of Massey Coal Company. Described as thirty times worse than the 1989 *Exxon Valdez* oil spill, the release of the sludge—which contained arsenic, mercury, and lead—contaminated the water supply for 27,000 people.[1] When the community wanted answers after the flood, the Environmental Protection Agency (EPA) held meetings at local churches. The EPA's representatives told the residents sitting in the pews that sludge from the flood was not harmful because "everything in the sludge was in the periodic table," said Mickey McCoy, a retired high-school English teacher from Inez, Kentucky.

"The coal-slurry flood opened my eyes to the fact that government agencies were not the watchdogs for the people," he said. "They were the guard dogs for the coal companies." His county experiences a hundred-year flood every eighteen months, Mickey said, and safe drinking water is not available from the taps. "They clear-cut the mountains, fill the valleys with the unprofitable materials, and cover the streams," he said. "They are bombing the mountains" (fig. 6.1). By 2007, 25 percent of the land area in Martin County had been stripped by mountaintop removal.[2]

Mickey spoke directly to the role of faith communities as bearing witness to the impacts of mountaintop removal. "You have the capacity to reach people in your churches and synagogues," he said. Mickey attends Golden Memorial United Methodist Church, where many people have connections through their jobs or family to mountaintop removal mining. "I feel people in the church don't feel it's their responsibility," he said. "If it's not their responsibility, whose

Figure 6.1 Christians are responding to the injustices of mountaintop removal, a mining practice with devastating ecological and health impacts on communities in Appalachia. Flight provided by SouthWings www.southwings.org. Photo by the author.

is it?" With this question, he raised his palms in the air, making an appeal to those seated in the room.

Mickey was talking to a gathering of people of faith who had traveled on a pilgrimage from the mountains of western North Carolina, along the Appalachian mountain chain, to coal country in eastern Kentucky. Organized by the religious environmental organization North Carolina Interfaith Power & Light, the pilgrimage was designed for an interfaith group to experience firsthand the devastating impacts of mountaintop removal on God's land and people. The trip would culminate in reflection, prayer, and action in congregations back home, whose demand for coal helps to fuel the mining industry.

This journey, coordinated with the grassroots organization Kentuckians for the Commonwealth, engaged faith communities in witnessing a mining practice that blows off the entire top of a mountain to gain access to the coal seams below.[3] This practice results in the dumping of mining wastes into streams, with devastating ecological and health impacts to the communities below. Indeed, mining waste has covered 2,000 miles of streams in Appalachia, and nearly 500 mountains have been destroyed by mountaintop removal.[4]

A pilgrimage is a journey for spiritual enrichment that involves travel to a place of meaning. As such, this experience often involves encounters with new places, uncertainty, and the unknown. As people of faith, our traditions are rich with stories of pilgrimage, as when Abraham sought the presence of God in the desert. Traditional destinations for such journeys in the Christian faith include the birthplace of Jesus and the site of the passion and the resurrection in the Holy Land. A pilgrimage has the power to bring diverse people, beliefs, and faith traditions together around a sacred site based in a community.[5]

In resolutions by diverse denominations against mountaintop removal, people of faith have described the practice as a "blight on God's creation."[6] An article entitled "This Little (Coal-Fired) Light of Mine" highlights a candlelight prayer vigil by Christians in front of the White House to advocate for an end to mountaintop removal practices in Appalachia.[7] But too many congregations are unaware of the impacts of mountaintop removal on the people of Appalachia and the role of our demand for coal in this environmental crisis.

The journey described in this chapter involved twelve pilgrims—from faith communities including Episcopalian, United Church of Christ, and Jewish—in an encounter with mountaintop removal that included flying over the mountains, hiking on mining sites, praying with local ministers, and scattering wildflower seeds on mined earth. The spiritual journey revealed lessons for other faith communities: connecting pilgrimages with sacred places, working with local organizations, creating an immersion experience, using prayer as a grounding force, hearing testimonies of faith, and reflecting on feelings and actions.

Sacred Objects, Pilgrims, and Places

Every pilgrimage includes a beginning and an end, but often the travel in between provides the context for the story. To begin this journey, twelve pilgrims met at the office of the Episcopal Diocese of Western North Carolina to introduce themselves and load their backpacks and suitcases into the white van of the Church of the Advocate, which ministers to the homeless community in Asheville, North Carolina. The four-hour drive took this group through four states: North Carolina, Tennessee, Virginia, and, finally, Kentucky. The van traversed Appalachia, passing and crossing rolling green mountains with bright blue skies and thick white clouds above.

One of the pilgrims, Maureen, shared her experiences working as a community organizer in the 1960s in the coalfields of Tennessee and Virginia, where families faced malnutrition due to poverty, homes covered in soot, unemployment, and black lung disease from the mines. "The odd person in the hollers [hollows] were the ones who were employed, and they all depended on the mines," she said. Maureen described mining as the cultural stamp of the communities, where miners received certificates to buy staples at the company store, increasing their dependence on the coal companies. As Harry Caudill wrote in *Night Comes to the Cumberlands*, "Coal has always cursed the land in which it lies."[8] This group of pilgrims drove along U.S. 23 through Tennessee and Virginia, passing the road to Artisan Well Hollow, a community where Maureen once worked. The four-lane road bypassed the small towns and former mine camps in Appalachia, rural centers now cut off from major traffic.

The sloping mountains, the agricultural areas in the valleys, and the Walmarts provided the visual backdrop for the journey along the Country Music Highway in Kentucky. About twenty miles outside of Hazard, Kentucky, trucks filled with black coal barreled down both sides of the road. Along Kentucky Route 160, the van passed the first sign of mountaintop removal, a green slurry-like lake with a mountain of gravel above, standing isolated between two green mountaintops. The mountaintop had been blown off to access the coal, leaving the inside of the mountain as an artifact of its previous existence. The flattened mountain resembled a raised moonscape between two gentle green slopes.

The destination and base camp for the pilgrimage was the Hindman Settlement School, a center established in 1902 for progressive education and community service and located on Troublesome Creek in Hindman, Kentucky. The back of the van was filled with five-gallon jugs of water, which group members carted into the dining room and bunk rooms at the school. While the pilgrims could drink water straight from the taps in Asheville, the drinking water was not safe in this community because of the impacts of mining. In some places in eastern Kentucky and western Virginia, families were warned to avoid bathing in the local water as well.

Seated in a circle of rocking chairs on the front porch of the Hindman Settlement School, the travelers reintroduced themselves, their faith backgrounds, and their reasons for embarking on this three-day pilgrimage. The introductory letter from North Carolina Interfaith Power & Light had asked everyone to bring one sacred object that reflected their connection to faith and the sacredness of the natural world. As members of the group rocked back and forth in their chairs at sunset, they presented the sacred objects and told their stories, placing each object in the center of the circle.

Former FBI agent Avery Rollins, who spoke with a soft Mississippi accent, explained that he was reared Southern Baptist but now worshipped as an Episcopalian. Avery held up a light brown, chiseled knife that looked like an arrowhead. Holding the knife in his hand, he said that, growing up on a farm, he spent endless hours walking along a river and in the woods. "I have heard discussion of thin places," he said, "places where you are a step away from the divine. I find those thin places in the woods, creeks, and farms where I found this knife."

With deep smile lines framing his eyes, Kevin Pentz, an organizer with Kentuckians for the Commonwealth, presented a silver lighter owned by his grandfather, a deep miner in Pennsylvania. His grandfather's job was to measure the depth and width of the mine, and he used the lighter to light his headlamp. "They had to grab him by his feet and pull him out of the mine," said Kevin. "And he could feel the roof pushing down on him." One day, Kevin's grandfather walked off the job and never returned. But he ran for office as the recorder of deeds in western Pennsylvania. Kevin showed the group the words "Recorder of Deeds" engraved on the lighter, as he placed it amid the other sacred objects. His grandfather died of black lung disease a week before Kevin was born, so Kevin heard these stories from his grandmother after he began his work with mining communities in eastern Kentucky. Grounding this pilgrimage in a sense of the sacred allowed the group to share their personal connections to God and the earth before exploring those threads in eastern Kentucky.

Visiting a Community Affected by Mountaintop Removal

By design, a pilgrimage takes people out of their own communities and places them in the role of visitor, whether the journey stretches thousands, hundreds, or only a few miles. At dinner the first night, several members of the group brought up the importance of sensitivity to the cultures and communities in Kentucky. Kevin responded to the question of how to enter a community by saying that the most important aspect is to acknowledge that you are a visitor. "That shields you from doing a lot of damage," he said. "The problem comes when you don't acknowledge that you are not from here." The community members who work with Kentuckians for the Commonwealth are usually happy to have others observe mountaintop removal and validate the reality of the problems. "The coal company is telling them that the water smells like eggs from methane, not from mining," Kevin said. "Government officials and inspectors are constantly saying the problem isn't real."

Kentuckians for the Commonwealth facilitates these tours so that visitors can meet with real people affected by mountaintop removal and hear their insights, rather than only see the destruction. It also organizes tours for local communities, so people in Harlan County, for example, get to visit with residents in Floyd County who are experiencing the same problems. "People are often limited in their space," he said. "They grew up in this holler but may not realize that mountaintop removal impacts this entire region." In these gentle mountains, Kevin explained, people identify themselves by hollows, the narrow valleys surrounded by hillsides where they live. This pilgrimage placed a high priority on working with local organizations, like Kentuckians for the Commonwealth, with deep connections to the communities affected by mountaintop removal.

Mountaintop removal mining differs from deep mining as the coal companies blow off the tops of the mountains to expose the coal seams, rather than extracting the coal from inside the mountain—a far more expensive method. The major coal companies working in eastern Kentucky include International Coal Group (ICG), Peabody, Consolidated, and TECO Coal Corporation. Mountaintop removal results in sludge ponds, which are supposed to hold the remnants of the mining. The problem comes with flooding and erosion, as the ponds' dams break loose, causing water and sludge to flow into homes and schools. One poster protesting the impacts of a sludge flood stated, "God didn't flood us. TECO did." It is not surprising that the counties with the most surface mining are also the poorest counties.

The explosion of mountaintops forms long, wide mesas that resemble desert topography. In this area of eastern Kentucky, the 300-million-year-old mountains are all about the same height, worn down from the time the Appalachians were the size of the Himalayas. The geological structure means that the rock layers are about at the same level, so coal companies can "peel back" the rock layers to get to the seams of coal.

Mountaintop removal most directly affects the people of West Virginia, Kentucky, Virginia, and Tennessee. The radical form of strip mining begins by clearing the topsoil and vegetation on the tops of mountains, often by burning the trees or burying them in valleys.[9] Accessing the coal within the mountain can demand the removal of as much as 800 feet of elevation, using explosives that blast the communities below the ridgelines, often damaging the foundations of homes and wells. Massive equipment, such as draglines standing twenty-two stories high, haul away the rubble, or "spoil," which is dumped in the valleys, streams, and forests below. The washed coal is then shipped to coal-fired power plants, while the excess from the treatment, which contains toxins such as mercury and arsenic, is stored in sludge or slurry ponds. The reclamation efforts typically involve hydroseeding, spraying a mixture of non-native grass seeds, mulch, and fertilizer on the disturbed topsoil with no measures to restore aquifers or forests.[10]

In eastern Kentucky, Kentuckians for the Commonwealth (KFTC) began its grassroots efforts in 1981 with about thirty people from five different counties. The acronym KFTC first stood for Kentucky Fair Tax Coalition. The original organizers realized that the coal companies owned a majority of the wealth in the region but were paying almost no taxes. "One coal company was paying the amount of tax on minerals equivalent to the taxes on a pickup truck," said Kevin. The group soon realized that most people in Kentucky were concerned with an issue called a broad form deed, rather than with taxes. In the late 1800s and early 1900s, before the advent of strip mining, coal companies bought a majority of mineral rights through broad form deeds, which gave the owner of the deed the right to extract minerals by whatever means possible.

Kevin described coal companies that showed up and told the landowner they had a right to bulldoze property and extract coal. "They even bulldozed cemeteries," he said. As he talked, he showed images from the region, including a picture of a coal truck with "Jesus is Lord" emblazoned on the side. Books such as *Strange as This Weather Has Been* and *Bringing Down the Mountains* give some insight into this world of ecological and cultural loss, where mountaintop removal results in flooding, health risks, degraded streams and forests, displaced families, and the loss of safe drinking water.[11] In this context, members of Kentuckians for the Commonwealth lobbied for the passage of an amendment to the state constitution that would prohibit coal companies from bulldozing someone's property. The amendment passed with 82 percent of the vote, one of the first big successes of this organization.

Kentuckians for the Commonwealth is a member organization with 6,000 members, who each pay an annual fee ranging from $15 to $60, based on income and need. The organization works on such diverse issues as mining, tax reform, economic development, and voter registration; it boasts six chapters in eastern Kentucky, which includes twelve major coal-producing counties. The group has advocated for both state and federal legislation involving mountaintop removal. In 2008, for example, the organization worked to introduce the Stream Saver Bill (SB 139, HB 416) to the House of Representatives in the Kentucky legislature. This bill would prohibit coal companies from burying streams with the waste from mining, On the federal level, its members advocated for the Clean Water Protection Act (H.R. 1310), which in 2009 had 154 co-sponsors for this bill that directly targets the impacts of mountaintop removal on water. In 2009, Kentuckians for the Commonwealth lobbied legislators when the U.S. Senate held its first hearings on mountaintop removal in discussions of the Appalachian Restoration Act (S. 696).

With a laptop computer, Kevin took the group of pilgrims on a virtual flyover of mountaintop removal, using Google Earth images to project the locations of the surface mining sites. He first focused on Martin County, which was almost completely mined in the 1980s. The 1970s saw the proliferation of contour mining, which creates a "bench" in the mountain, exposes the seam of coal, and pushes the excess dirt and rocks to the other side. As the machinery got larger, coal companies gained the ability to take the whole mountain, rather than expose only one side.

The agency in charge of regulation here is the Kentucky Division of Mine Reclamation and Enforcement. "There are state regulations as long as the inspector is standing there, but if the inspector is not there, there are no state regulations," Kevin said. Several members of the group asked about the regulation of water quality, as we each carried a bottle with water brought from Asheville. "I have only one thing to say—don't drink the water. Don't drink the water. You can drink it, but it's at your own risk," he said. Indeed, we learned that some community members drink coffee, rather than water. They believe heating the water reduces the negative health impacts of water from the tap.

An Immersion Experience: Seeing the
Mountains from the Air

Almost any documentary about mountaintop removal includes video recordings of flying above the Appalachian Mountains in a small plane to view the devastation firsthand. After seeing mountaintop removal sites on a similar pilgrimage, Old Testament scholar Ellen Davis likened the destruction to an "environmental Auschwitz," reflecting on the desecration of hundreds of mountains, forests, and streams. The conservation organization SouthWings, based in Asheville, sponsors many of these flyovers; its volunteer pilots give their time for biological monitoring, education, and outreach, all from the perspective of a small four-seater plane.

Fog hovered over the ridgelines and hollows as the van drove to the Wendell Ford regional airport in Perry County. The pilgrims passed a sign that announced, "We love our coal miners." The drive took the group past towns with names like Dwarf and Rowdy, as well as past signs announcing "Blasting Zone: 1,000 feet." In Bonnyman, Kentucky, a farmer sold green beans and tomatoes in front of the Second Creek Church of Christ. While we drove past these small towns, the mountaintop removal sites stood just above the ridgeline, often invisible from the roads below.

The view from outside the airport provided a startling glimpse into mountaintop removal from the ground: blasted hilltops surrounded the airport. The inside of the airport reflected a public relations campaign for mining with four posters announcing "Coal Mining: Our Future," which included bright photos of reclaimed mine sites and reseeded mountaintops. The photographs depicted the flattened mountains as new homes for golf courses, houses, four-wheeler trails, airports, and wildlife. Near the picturesque photos, dozens of gallons of bottled water sat on the floor of a small meeting room.

The small blue-and-white plane soon arrived to take the first group of three passengers, while the other participants watched a segment of the religious environmental film *Renewal*, featuring faith leaders on a similar flyover and journey to explore mountaintop removal. In the documentary, evangelical author Matthew Sleeth described his experience of seeing the mountains from the air: "The first word that comes to mind—as a Christian and a doctor—is rape."[12] Allen Johnson, with the group Christians for the Mountains, recalled a community member who had been bathing her three-year-old child in the tap water from her home and later discovered the water contained arsenic.

After viewing the film, the pilgrims sat in a circle to reflect on the images of mountaintop removal. Some expressed anger that politicians could ignore this story. "It's beyond me how political leaders can hear these stories of people affected by mountaintop removal and not do anything," said Avery. Others who had seen the film at previous events described the power of the scenes and the words expressed by the faith leaders. "I've seen this several times, and I still want to cry," said Maureen, with tears welling up in her eyes. "And we need to cry. We need to grieve." As an ordained United Church of Christ minister, Leah McCullough called on the power of religion. "The only way to get extensive change in the South is through the churches," she said. With this charge, the second group of passengers, including me, loaded into the small plane.

From the air, the mine sites looked like a criminal onslaught against the land. As the plane lifted, the aerial view revealed flattened mountains, virtual moonscapes, in every direction, with houses and silted streams at the base of the mining sites. The coal trucks moving from one place to the next looked like small Tonka trucks on the ground, as the airplane passed over the ICG mine Starfire. The pilot flew over a massive sludge pond, an unlined reservoir for debris. Some of the mountaintop removal sites were green, hydroseeded to resemble a golf course setting in a sea of forests and valleys. Other sites exposed the orange, yellow, and tan shades of the dirt, like isolated mesas amid the trees.

As the plane neared the ICG mine near Vicco, Kentucky, the pilot announced, "Most places you fly look pretty. This looks like a war zone." Returning to the airport, the plane flew over the town of Hazard, revealing postage-stamp-sized schools, yellow school buses, a Walmart, and a Lowe's—all surrounded by mountaintop removal sites. As the wheels of the airplane hit the ground, the pilot opened the door next to the passenger seat to circulate air. The pilgrims stepped out of the plane, leaving behind the view of the mesas of destruction.

Driving through Hazard, the van passed the Lowe's and the Walmart that had seemed so small from the plane. In 2005, miners with the American Blasting Company were blasting the area behind the Walmart to expose a coal seam. The explosion sent rocks crashing into the ceiling of the store, injuring three shoppers.[13] The Division of Explosives and Blasting issued seven citations, with a maximum fine of $1,000 each. Across town, a sludge pond sat above Hazard High School, which had an emergency action plan in case the pond broke. About fifteen miles past Hazard, the van passed the Sportsplex built on a flattened mountaintop; overall, less than 5 percent of the land flattened by mining was used for economic development.[14] One member of the group spied a bumper sticker that gave insight into the politics, power, and emotion around mountaintop removal: "Save a Miner. Shoot a Treehugger."

Planting Wildflowers in Prayer: A Vespers
Service on a Moonscape

The drive from the airport to the site of an afternoon hike and vespers service on a blasted mountaintop took the group through lush
green valleys dotted with small houses, mobile homes, and churches,
including the Philadelphia Old Regular Baptist Church. After driving for miles on winding roads through narrow hollows, the group
met Father John Rausch, a Catholic priest with decades of experience
organizing faith communities around mountaintop removal. In his
work with the Catholic Committee of Appalachia, Father Rausch
has led mountaintop removal tours for seminarians, local community
members, religious leaders, and interfaith groups.

The pilgrims formed a circle outside a one-story brown house
with four children's bicycles outside and a looming mountaintop removal site above. "This site is private property, and we have the owner's permission to be here," explained Father Rausch. "But on the
mountaintop removal site, it is leased property. If the coal company
wants to kick us off, they can." With this warning, the group began
hiking past a stream that ran by the home to a huge mountain of
gravel.

The route passed a pond below the mountaintop removal site,
with someone's fishing tackle left on the bank of the murky water.
The gravel road became steeper, revealing layers of bare earth with
no tree cover to provide shade. The hot afternoon sun baked the
group, and we soon gathered in a circle to hear Father Rausch proclaim, "Welcome to God's mountain, which someone has decided
to alter. What do you notice?" (fig. 6.2). One person pointed out the
deer tracks in the road leading to the site. Another drew attention
to a single tulip poplar growing in the midst of the rubble. "How
can they be permitted to do this?" someone asked. Above the
prayer circle, a procession of huge trucks transported the land into
the valley.

With the blazing sun above, Father Rausch read "Canticle of the
Sun" by St. Francis of Assisi from *Care for Creation: A Franciscan
Spirituality of the Earth*:[15]

Figure 6.2 Pilgrims hiked to a mountaintop removal site for prayers and a vespers service. Photo by the author.

Be praised, my Lord, through all your creatures, especially my lord Brother Sun, who brings the day; and you give light through him. And he is beautiful and radiant in all his splendor! Of you, Most High, he bears the likeness.

Be praised, my Lord, through Sister Moon and the stars; in the heavens you have made them, precious and beautiful.[16]

His polo shirt and baseball hat soaked with sweat, Father Rausch posed the question for us to answer in our home congregations: "What are we hearing from our religious traditions about these mining practices?"

The final prayers came from *At Home in the Web of Life*, a pastoral letter signed by Catholic bishops in this Appalachian region affected by mountaintop removal.[17] "These mountains are truly a holy place," Father Rausch read. Psalm 72:3 sets the tone for this document: "The mountains shall yield peace for the people, and the hills justice." Father Rausch then gave each member of the group a handful of wildflower seeds to scatter amid the rubble, a chance to bring life to an area of desecration and create personal prayers of healing and pledges of action. Each person walked to a place of solitude and threw the seeds into the dry, hot earth.

After the service, seven members of the group decided to scramble up the steep incline to catch a glimpse of the coal equipment and to see the view from the top. Will Harlan, a Buddhist and writer, who had raced with the Tarahumara Indians in Copper Canyon, Mexico, sprinted up the rocks, while others stepped more gingerly on the shifting rubble and sand. At the top, these adventurers realized that the destruction continued as far as they could see. "The wasteland just kept going and going, one false peak after another," said Leah. "There is no top," echoed Will. "Only piles and piles and endless piles of rock."

As they scaled the first peak of rocks, five massive coal trucks had roared past them, with one driver reaching for a radio, perhaps to alert the coal company of their presence. "I didn't know whether to run and hide or wave, but there was nowhere to hide," said Leah, the ordained minister. "So I just waved." Within minutes, a small pickup truck approached her, and the driver asked, "Are y'all leaving?" And they did. Back in the van, Avery's wife, Jackie, reflected on the experience of praying while standing on the rubble above people's homes. "It feels like the coal company has no value for the people, the culture," she said. "Just like the rocks, the people have been pushed away." After climbing into the van, each person drank from a water bottle—containing the clean water brought from another state.

Testimonies of Faith: The Power of Local Stories

That evening, the pilgrims gathered in a meeting room with colorful quilts on the walls to hear the testimonies of faith leaders who have been fighting mountaintop removal. The facilitator for the evening, Randy Wilson, brought his banjo and his theological background to the circle of local pastors and pilgrims. Wearing a baseball cap and singing with a sweet Appalachian accent, Randy played his banjo and opened the discussion by reciting lines from Emily Dickinson: "It's all I have to bring today—This and my heart beside—This and my heart and all the fields and all the meadows wide." With this poetic opening, Randy asked the faith leaders who were members of Kentuckians for the Commonwealth to talk about their faith and their battles to save these mountains.

Truman Hurt   A pastor of the Kodak Church of Christ, Truman Hurt introduced himself as a disabled coal worker, later explaining that he suffered from black lung disease. In his church and community, Truman had spoken out against the impacts of mining. But representatives of the coal company insinuated that his son could be fired from his job at a gravel company if Truman continued to preach a message that did not support coal. An imposing man with a detached demeanor, Truman told the group that the water source for the church was near a coal mine, so parishioners had to carry bottled water to the church. "The creeks are stopped up," he said. "We've had houses flooded. If you have a hard rain, look out."

Truman explained that the seventeen miles between Hazard and his hometown of Vicco contained numerous hollows where people suffer from bad water. "Right is in the eyes of God," he said, raising his voice like a preacher. "Raping the land is just as bad as raping a woman. Right is right." After this bold statement, one of the women from our group, Jackie, spoke directly to Truman, pointing out the injustice of the fact that he gave up everything so that she could have energy in her home.

McKinley Sumner   The eldest community member in the circle, McKinley Sumner, held the floor with his lean, sinewy presence and talkative manner. While others sat in their chairs to talk, McKinley stood up in the middle of the circle, staking out his territory as speaker. He described how the ICG company trespassed to place oil and gas lines on his grandfather's property. The company then offered McKinley $95,000 to mine on his property. When he responded that he did not want any blasting at his doorstep, he was offered $200,000 and then $300,000, with the promise that he could live in his house until he died. They later offered him a house in Vicco if he would sign. "I was raised on this property, and I would not leave," he announced. One day, McKinley heard trees popping outside his house, so he put on his boots to investigate. "I saw a clearing and heard the monster—the bulldozers," he said.

From August 2006 to December 2007, McKinley fought ICG with the help of the Appalachian Citizens Law Center, as the coal company had taken some of his property and mined it without his permission. At a meeting in London, Kentucky, representatives from KFTC, the Sierra Club, and the coal company tried to resolve the situation. The coal company tried to get him to sign a thirteen-page document, which stipulated that he had no recourse if its employees trespassed on his property by mistake. "Their lawyers thought we were stupid," he said. "My sister said they were trying to shut her brother up. They will never shut my brother up, she said." As McKinley continued his tale from the center of the circle, Randy quietly strummed the banjo to signal a transition to the next testimony.

After McKinley took his seat, Randy stated in a hushed voice, "What a piece of shit we have made with something that is holy. This is a spiritual question to the core. What is holy?" He picked up his banjo and began singing a Jean Ritchie song: "Now is the cool of the day. / This earth is a garden, the garden of my Lord. / And he walks in the garden. / In the cool of the day." With this refrain, people joined in the song, clapping their hands, tapping their feet, with the release that spiritual music can provide. As the song ended, Randy reminded us that this song says that *now* is the cool of the day—not the future.

Melvin May Sitting with stoic expressions on their faces, Melvin and Etta May wore gray-and-white T-shirts emblazoned with the logo of Shelby United Methodist Church. When the time came for Melvin to speak, he told the group that his sister had encouraged him to come tonight, although he was not sure why he was here. The reason for his presence became clear as he talked with passion about his experience in Maytown, Kentucky, where generations of his family had lived for 225 years. "To see this destruction tears at your heart," he said, his voice gaining momentum, even as tears came to his eyes. He described the scene when heavy rains came to the area, moving three sludge ponds down Wilson's Creek into the community of Maytown. The flooding washed away trailers and homes in the town. He waded through water to try to keep the debris out of houses.

"We had seven feet, six inches of water in Maytown, higher than the hundred-year flood," he said. Melvin paused, breathing deeply before raising a finger to emphasize his next words. "If you take away one thing," he said, "the people in this region suffer not for want of food or education. We suffer because of mountaintop removal and the coal companies who put greed ahead of people." Melvin told us that the people's suffering should be the spiritual reason for stopping mountaintop removal.

This passionate plea prompted Truman to announce with a preacher's cadence that the world needed a revival like never before. "Many churches have become social clubs that want good dinners and entertainment preaching," he said. "We've got to turn back to God. Jesus is the way, the truth, and the light." Truman ended with this declaration: "Here in eastern Kentucky, we live by the golden rule. He who has the gold makes the rules."

After this fervent testimony, Avery, the former FBI agent, reminded the group of all the times people go to public meetings and sit quietly. "How many of us wake up the next day and wish we had said something?" he asked in a deep baritone voice that commanded attention. "Speak up. We are the people." As a closing, Randy strummed his banjo and led us in James Still's "A Song Shall Rise."

In that Resurrection morning, when the trumpet of God shall
    sound.
We shall rise, we shall rise.
Then the saints will come rejoicing, and no tears will e'er be
    found.
We shall rise, we shall rise.

During the singing, someone jumped up and started dancing. Another person embraced Truman in a sincere hug; half the group danced, while the other half hugged the community members who had shared their stories. This group of pilgrims came as outsiders, but the pastors and coal miners made us feel that we had a role in bearing witness to their struggles.

What Does My Faith Require of Me?
Reflection, Prayer, and Action

"I want to pull out the book of Lamentations and offer laments about what I am feeling," said Leah, opening the circle of reflection. The activist community, as a collective, often moves straight from an experience to action, without spending time on feelings or our grief about environmental degradation. As Wendell Berry said about mountaintop removal, "If you know that according to our greatest teachers, this neighborliness is expected of us, then you will grieve in knowing that we humans are destroying the earth."[18] The pilgrims' circle of reflection first focused on the emotions, including grief and anger, generated by the journey to eastern Kentucky.

The hike on the mountaintop removal site had stirred deeper feelings of betrayal than the flyover, said participant Don Miller. He described hiking to the top of the site and hearing the rumble of the coal trucks. "We saw the trucks dwarfing us. These trucks that seemed like Tonka trucks from the air were huge on the ground." Avery leaned forward in his rocking chair before speaking. "My basic reaction is intense anger toward this industry that will lie," he said. "This is the worst thing I've ever seen. I have to keep in check my darker, basic instincts in reaction to this experience." Someone reminded us that social activist Van Jones once remarked that you cannot work in social justice without a spiritual practice to help "hold the pain."

Jill Rios, the director of North Carolina Interfaith Power & Light, described her tendency to demonize the men driving the trucks, when in reality they were people and, often, people of faith too. "How can a deep spiritual practice help us? How can our theo-logical roots ground us?" she asked. Jill described a legislative visit that she made regarding climate change legislation in North Caro-lina. The legislator was uncooperative during the meeting until Jill posed this simple question: "What do you think about this issue as a person of faith?" That question totally shifted the conversation and allowed him to connect. "Our faith is something we hold that is different from people in the secular environmental movement," she said.

The reflection continued with readings from *The Green Bible*[19]—Psalm 88, a prayer for help and despondency, and Psalm 22, a plea for deliverance from suffering and hostility—and from *Earth Gospel: A Guide to Prayer for God's Creation.*[20] The final prayer was read by Alice Cohen and came from the Jewish tradition, an eco-Shabbat prayer.

The prayers led the group to reflect on action and commitments, to consider how the pilgrims could take this experience back to their congregations at home. "What does our faith require of us?" asked Jill. She described efforts at the national Interfaith Power & Light to make mountaintop removal a priority, as a strategy for engaging more congregations in advocacy. "Most denominations have resolu-tions on mountaintop removal, but not a lot are engaged in advocacy," she admitted. These resolutions do reveal that diverse denominations can unite around their opposition to mountaintop removal. As one example, the United Methodist Church states:

[T]he millions and millions of tons of earth and rock removed from the tops of mountains are dumped into the valleys next to these mountains, totally destroying the springs and headwaters of streams in the valleys, along with all plant and animal life in them, and . . . mountaintop removal mining, by destroying home places, is also destroying ancestral ground, sacred ground where generations after generations have lived, gone to church, married, made and birthed babies, taken family meals, slept in peace, died and been buried.[21]

Opportunities for turning these resolutions into action exist at the local, regional, and federal levels for individuals and congregations. People of faith have lobbied in support of climate legislation in Congress. Also, NC IPL has collected signatures from a hundred clergy on a letter to North Carolina senators to advocate for climate legislation. Interfaith Power & Light affiliates across the country support churches in engaging in action and in advocacy for legislation against mountaintop removal. The circle of twelve pilgrims brainstormed additional ideas, including advocating for energy conservation in congregations and adopting a resolution for a ban on mountaintop removal. Action items with a social justice angle included involvement in NC IPL's Project Energize to weatherize low-income homes using volunteer labor from congregations.

The group ended the list of action items with a pledge to meet in one month to review progress and a benediction, "Go in Peace":

And now, I am supposed to say to you, "Go in peace." But how can I say, "Go in peace," when you are going out into a world where you are insecure, whether at home or on your neighborhood street?

—Out into a world where race is set against race and ethnic cleansing is a name for genocide?

—Out into a world where people are hungry and homeless, out of work and out of money, while their governments and corporate powers spend billions of dollars on what does not bring healing and growth, but destruction and death?

With a world like that out there, how can I say to you, "Go in peace?"

But I dare to say, "Go in peace," because Jesus says, "I give you my peace."

But remember, he who says, "I give you my peace" also says, "If you would be my disciple and [thereby] have my peace, take up your cross and follow me!"

So I dare to say, "Go in peace!"—if you dare!

And may we all say, "Amen!"[22]

The drive home on Highway 15 included a detour to a preserve located along this Kentucky Scenic Bypass, which had been saved from mountaintop removal by its unique geology. After a weekend of bearing witness to destruction, the group embraced the opportunity to hike on lush green trails by a flowing creek with clear water, undisturbed by mining. At the Bad Branch State Nature Preserve, the travelers loaded sack lunches into daypacks and headed out, eager to walk along trails in the canopy of trees, with tulip poplars and rocks the size of small houses lining the trail. After one mile, we came to a waterfall, crashing down from the rocks. Several members of the group stood on the rocks, letting the cascade of water flow over their bodies. This water would not harm anyone. Standing under the water, Will raised his arms and held them under the water's flow. At the end of the hike, Alice remarked, "I didn't realize how much I needed to move my body as a response to the despair." And may we all say, "Amen."

Making a Pilgrimage as Ministry: Lessons Learned

A pilgrimage presents a tangible opportunity to immerse members of a congregation in an environmental issue and explore the communities affected by it. This three-day journey to bear witness to mountaintop removal reveals concrete lessons for other churches seeking to integrate the environment into this traditional ministry.

Begin a pilgrimage with a connection to sacred spaces.

Ultimately, a pilgrimage connected with the environment is as much about spiritual growth as about stewardship of God's earth. Rituals can place the sacred as a priority in the journey. During the trip to eastern Kentucky, the ritual of sharing sacred objects allowed participants to share their personal stories of faith and the environment with each other, creating a narrative that tied them together. During the three days, the pilgrims placed those sacred objects at the center of the discussion circles as reminders of the importance of the sacred to environmental work.

Work with local organizations connected with local environmental issues.

Working with local organizations, either secular or religious, is often key to interacting with people and places outside your own community. Even a local pilgrimage that involves a different demographic from your own congregation should tap into the expertise and networks of community members. Kentuckians for the Commonwealth had invested years building relationships with its members, the pastors, the coal miners, and the landowners affected by the coal industry. These connections allowed the group to enter the community as respected visitors, rather than unwelcome tourists.

Provide an immersion experience, a firsthand education in an environment.

For people of faith, a pilgrimage is different from a book group or a prayer group since it provides an immersion experience, a spiritual "dunking" into a new environment. For these three days, participants on the mountaintop removal tour lived and breathed the mountains of eastern Kentucky, including the music of Randy Wilson's banjo and the rubble beneath their feet at mining sites. Pilgrimage as experiential education involves opportunities for this type of concrete experience, as well as chances to reflect, generalize, and plan for action.[23]

Integrate prayer and worship into the pilgrimage, in both healthy and degraded environments.

The central role of religion makes a spiritual journey different from a tour. Setting that tone through prayer and worship reminds participants of the foundation of the journey. Resources for sacred rituals, texts, and prayers during this pilgrimage included *The Green Bible; Earth Gospel: A Guide to Prayer for God's Creation; Care for Creation: A Franciscan Spirituality of the Earth*; and *Earth Prayers from around the World.*[24] Even with these resources, however, the evaluations from participants of this weekend revealed that they wanted additional prayer and worship integrated into the experience. One strategy for accomplishing this goal is to have an ordained person as one of the facilitators to integrate worship into the pilgrimage, in addition to the activities and interactions in the community.

Bear witness to testimonies of faith and share the power of local stories.

For many people, the most powerful aspect of the weekend was the discussion with local faith leaders about the impact of mountaintop removal on their lives. Hearing these pastors and community leaders speak from their hearts about the devastation moved many of us to tears. The bluegrass and gospel tunes sung together moved participants to dance. The hope that came from their stories provided a template for both inspiration and action. Seeing the mountaintop removal sites without hearing the testimonies of local people would have resulted in a flat experience, without the depth and complexity from the personal stories.

Offer opportunities to share emotions, prayers, reflections, and actions at home.

Bearing witness to environmental challenges that affect us all demands emotional engagement. In the environmental field, we often move straight from experience to action, posing the immediate question:

What can we do now? A pilgrimage should provide the chance to process emotions through prayer and reflection. The mountaintop removal pilgrimage generated a range of emotions: grief, anger, and frustration. Sharing those feelings set the stage for the next steps and strategies to be taken with congregations back home and with policy makers. Indeed, as a result of this trip, the North Carolina National Council of Churches issued a resolution calling for a ban in the state on the use of coal from mountaintop removal.

On Reflection

Don't drink the water.

As we lugged the five-gallon jugs of water from the van, I still could not believe that whole communities across Appalachia had unsafe drinking water. Rachel Rasmussen, one of my environmental education students from Warren Wilson College, had worked that summer of 2009 to help organize the mountaintop removal tour with North Carolina Interfaith Power & Light. Rachel recognized the irony of organizing an environmental pilgrimage to a toxic site that required the purchase of water bottled in plastic jugs. For almost five years, I lived in countries without access to safe water sources, but in this instance I traveled only four hours from my hometown to hear the admonition: Don't drink the water.

The households affected by the leaching of toxins into their water supply often cannot afford to buy bottled water for their families. As we heard, some people believe boiling the water eliminates the contaminants, so they drink coffee, rather than water. And even worse, in some communities, bathing in this same water may be toxic as well. As a mother of two daughters, I spend much of my evenings trying to get my kids into the bath. But how would I feel if I knew that putting my daughters into bathwater was hurting them?

While flying over the mountaintop removal sites, I had one thought: This can't be real. I felt as if I were in a science fiction movie, a surreal video of dry moonscapes next to verdant hilltops. As a teacher at Warren Wilson, I have seen scores of documentaries about mountaintop removal and heard dozens of speakers address the topic. My students are engaged in advocacy against mountaintop removal and coal-fired power plants. One student created a documentary about the sludge pond above the Marsh Fork Elementary School in West Virginia; another dressed up as a polar bear and chained herself to the gates of the proposed expansion of the Cliffside Power Plant near Shelby, North Carolina.

So I thought I knew what I was getting myself into. But I was wrong. I literally could not speak into the microphone on my headset in the plane. The devastation was everywhere—360 degrees of destroyed earth amid a patchwork of green hills. For me, part of the challenge was returning home to our mountains in western North Carolina, where I knew I could drive or hike to the mountaintop without encountering blasted earth hidden above the tree line. In Appalachia, 500 mountains have been destroyed by this type of mining, which endangers the lives of the families that live below the ridges. With such knowledge, it's hard for me to "go in peace."

A powerful moment of hope came for me at the end of our meeting with faith leaders Truman Hurt and Melvin May, when Randy Wilson's banjo played as locals and visitors hugged each other and danced in the middle of a circle of folding chairs. During the evening, we listened, prayed, and sang. And some force propelled us to hug each other as a physical act of connection between God's people. For me, that was prayer, a force greater than our individual intentions. And that prayer gives courage for us to go in peace—if we dare.

7

Educating Youth

Solar Panels at Camp, Creation Care at Sunday School

Keep these words that I am commanding you today in your heart. Recite them to your children and talk about them when you are at home and when you are away, when you lie down and when you rise.

—Deuteronomy 6:6–7 (NRSV)

Children are part of something bigger. They are a part of an age-old process where the sun rises, and the moon rises. Children will have hard times, and we can't predict when that will happen. But we can foster that innate connection to nature, which is one way you find your spiritual path.

—Vicki Garlock, Jubilee Community Church

The dining hall of the Mountain Trail Outdoor School hummed with the sound of controlled chaos as 150 middle-school students and their 20 adult chaperones ate lunch. Kids collected plastic cups, scraped the food off plates, and stacked the plates on the round wooden tables in the dining hall. During their first of two days at this environmental education program, the students from Charlotte, North Carolina, practiced the camp's protocols for cleaning up after meals. As they cleared the tables, students brought their uneaten food waste to the compost bin, staffed by instructor Rich Bowerman, who gave ten-second informal lessons on using food scraps for compost in the camp garden.

At the end of the meal, he hung the compost bucket from a scale that showed a total weight of eight pounds. The staff would use this information to increase awareness about food waste at the next meal. After the cleanup, director LeeAnne Martin announced the afternoon classes—a mountain ecology hike, canoeing and bog study, a high ropes course, and cooperation games—each taught in three-hour blocks on the campus of Kanuga Conferences in Hendersonville, North Carolina.

The Mountain Trail Outdoor School reaches 6,000 schoolchildren a year as a residential environmental education program of Kanuga Conferences, which is affiliated with the Episcopal Church. This program represents one example of how churches have integrated the environment into the ministry of educating youth. The Kanuga story reflects the importance of engaging youth in the outdoors, whether they are studying the diversity of a mountain bog or following food waste from the lunch table to the garden. The educational ministry of Kanuga also reveals the challenges and opportunities of maintaining camp facilities, like water heaters and dining halls, that reflect environmental values in tight economic times.

This chapter addresses the question of how Christian education can engage youth in environmental stewardship. At its heart, Christian education promotes discipleship, building a lifelong love of God in a supportive environment with peers and adult mentors. Seminaries have master's programs in Christian education ministry to train faith leaders in this mission. Countless curricula exist for Christian education for children, including the *Journey to Adulthood*[1] program for middle- and high-school students and *Godly Play* for preschoolers.[2] But what are churches doing on the ground to connect Christian education for young people with the moral imperative to protect God's earth?

The Reverend Fletcher Harper, executive director of GreenFaith, said that one of the greatest needs in the religious environmental movement is for stories, strategies, and materials that integrate the environment into religious education for youth. "That is one question we hear over and over," he said. "People want to know how others are connecting the environment to youth. They want resources to use in Sunday schools and youth groups." This chapter provides a response to that need through the stories of faith leaders such as Stan Hubbard, the president of Kanuga Conferences, who saw green initiatives for camps as a discernment process that led to the installation of one of the largest solar water-heating systems in the Southeast (fig. 7.1). Another story features the ministry of Vicki Garlock, who rewrote a Sunday

Figure 7.1 Kanuga Conferences incorporates environmentalism into its programming and facilities, such as its solar water-heating system. Photo by Kanuga Conferences, Inc.

school curriculum to integrate creation spirituality across all grade levels. Last, communications professor Maria Roca, a lifelong Catholic, targeted today's teens by creating eco-parables on DVD that promote environmental stewardship from a religious perspective.

The stories in this chapter highlight the ministry of Christian education for youth in three contexts: camps and conference centers, Sunday school classes, and youth groups. The lessons for congregations and Christian educators include using land owned by religious institutions to engage youth in the outdoors, ensuring that camp facilities reflect environmental stewardship, using facilities as a teaching tool, integrating creation into Sunday school, and harnessing the power of relevant media to promote environmentally responsible behaviors.

God's Land and People: Connecting Youth to the Outdoors

Combining natural history with practical facts, instructor Jane Vogelman stopped on the trail to show a witch hazel plant to the middle-school hikers at the Mountain Trail Outdoor School. After Jane explained that many skin care products contain witch hazel, the students rubbed a witch hazel leaf over their faces, from their foreheads to their chins. As the hike continued, Jane used stories and questions to engage the students in the forest and mountains around them. To introduce the pileated woodpecker, she explained that the design of the first football helmet relied on studies of the woodpecker's skull. For a discussion on decomposers, she used the letters F-B-I to stand for the *f*ungus, *b*acteria, and *i*nsects that break down, or decompose, wood and leaves along the forest floor. In response, several boys began to notice what they called "CFMs," or cool funky mushrooms in bright reds, yellows, and whites.

Religious camps and conference centers provide a valuable context for introducing youth to God's great world, particularly given the documented decrease in the amount of time children in the United States spend outdoors. Richard Louv's book *Last Child in the Woods*—used by thousands of teachers, health professionals, and camp directors—synthesizes relevant research on the importance of outdoor play to the physical, emotional, and cognitive development of children.[3] In comparison to children growing up in previous generations, today's youth as a whole spend significantly fewer hours outdoors, especially in unstructured play such as climbing trees, exploring gullies, or digging holes in the mud.

Louv presents multiple reasons for this decline, including unsubstantiated fears of child abduction, promoted by the media, and the loss of green spaces due to development. Many children today hear repeated messages in schools and from the media about environmental destruction, without developing a foundation of caring for landscapes, which often begins with simple play outdoors. In response to this research, educators have begun a movement called No Child Left Inside, which includes federal legislation for environmental education in the schools.[4]

The environmental education work of the fifteen-year-old Mountain Trail Outdoor School ties into the mission of Kanuga: "to provide for God's people in this broken world a glimpse of the Kingdom through hearing the Gospel, experiencing Christian community, and being empowered for strength, growth, and service in both our individual communities and in the rest of God's creation."[5] While the focus is secular, the programs at the Mountain Trail Outdoor School teach children about healthy human and ecological communities. The activities also connect with the religious programs that church-affiliated schools conduct during their visit. During their experience, students stay from three to five days in cabins, eat family-style, work in the dining hall, and immerse themselves in the ecology of the Kanuga campus, forests, trails, and garden.

The classes are divided into two broad categories—environmental and adventure—with fourteen seasonal staff and two permanent staff as instructors. A typical three-day session includes forest ecology, pond and stream ecology, rock climbing, team-building games, a night hike, and evening campfires. Most schools conduct fundraising events to cover the cost of the program.

At religious camps, the traditional camp season in the summer engages both campers and staff with religious teachings and the local environment, in effect teaching about "God's two books—the Bible and the outdoors."[6] Many camps and conference centers such as Kanuga also operate secular environmental education programs for schools as a strategy for extending outreach and education beyond campers of their denomination. These programs promote utilization of the camp and its educational programs in the academic year between summer camping seasons.

The Mountain Trail Outdoor School was started with a few small school groups attending the conference center when the center did not have camp groups. For camps interested in initiating residential environmental education programs, director LeeAnne Martin advised starting with a small season of three to four seed groups with contract staff. "Have the groups close together, as a bumper before or after your summer sessions," she recommended. "Begin to show the viability of filling in gaps in the camp season." Mountain Trail Outdoor School now pulls students from eight states, and participating schools are as far away as New Orleans and as close as Asheville, just twenty miles north.

The challenges faced by the program include the seasonal employment of instructors: LeeAnne hires staff for the fall or spring season; programming runs from August through November and from February through May. Despite that typical challenge, she had to hire only one new instructor in fall 2009 because the others were returning staff, many of them graduates of the program. "I would love to offer year-round work with benefits, but that's not the nature of residential environmental education programming," she said. Her instructors make $250–$280 a week, lead instructors make $285–$315, and coordinators make $320–$350, plus room, board, and major medical insurance.

Reared in the Baptist faith in eastern Kentucky, LeeAnne said that the environment is her church. "We were on a backpacking trip during a summer camp session when one girl asked me if I believed in God," she remembered. "I asked her to look around at the forest and tell me how you can't believe in God." LeeAnne gets her greatest sense of accomplishment from the stories of campers, such as the one who came by that day to explain that he wanted to return as a staff member in the future. She shared other stories of students overcoming their fears on the climbing tower or experiencing profound moments of reflection in the woods.

Greening Facilities with Creative Approaches to Financing

The long-range planning process for Kanuga includes many initiatives started by the Mountain Trail Outdoor School staff, such as starting a recycling center and expanding the garden created by instructor Jane Vogelman. "I saw a disconnect between what we were teaching and what we were eating," Jane said, as she worked in the organic garden, adorned with prayer flags flying over the beds of basil, bell peppers, and green tomatoes during the early fall. She left Kanuga to work at several farms and then came back to implement what she learned. Jane took a beekeeping class and started keeping bees at the garden. She also installed a rain barrel to capture rainwater to use for irrigation, each small action helping to create facilities that reflect environmental values.

Kanuga president Stan Hubbard has developed a pithy catchphrase: "Environmental stewardship is in Kanuga's DNA." He has repeated that phrase in press releases, newsletter articles, and brochures to drive home the message that the green initiatives connect to both the history and the mission of this camp and conference center. Dressed in seersucker pants and a white Kanuga polo shirt, Stan led the staff with the crisp, articulate manner of a business professional. But his open and engaging style fit the environment of a camp and conference center in the business of spiritual growth and fun.

The modern stories of greening Kanuga connect to its history of conservation. Between 1905 and 1909, the dam at Kanuga Lake produced hydroelectric power, and the staff milled wood and built furniture from trees on the 1,400-acre grounds. The historic Chapel of the Transfiguration, along with the pews, altar, and liturgical furniture, was built with wood felled during an ice storm in 1936.[7] Stan credited his current staff with pushing the camp and conference center so that the facilities reflect the environmental curriculum. The faculty at the Mountain Trail Outdoor School was struggling when he came to Kanuga in 2005, he said, because of the lack of connection between what they taught in the woods and on the lake and what the campers saw in the facilities. Stan encouraged the instructors to look for environmental initiatives that would have the largest impact and would be visible to the community.

With this prompting, a staff member at the Mountain Trail Outdoor School took on the responsibility of conducting research on the possibility of solar water heating at Kanuga. In 2006, the staff decided to undertake a pilot test using solar panels to heat water at one of the camper cabins. "We decided to start small, conduct analysis, and see how much energy we really saved," said Stan. "We discovered two things. First, it worked. And second, the solar panels created a teachable moment for campers and staff." The panels were installed at a part of the campus that houses the Mountain Trail Outdoor School during the school year and a specialized summer camp. "Together, those two programs bring an incredibly diverse array of kids, and they were all interested in the solar panels, curious about how they worked," he told me. "The staff became more enthusiastic about their jobs. It was like lighting a fire under our programs." This small greening project became a transformative initiative for the entire camp and conference center.

With a background in finance, Stan kept brainstorming options about financing an expansion to Kanuga's solar water-heating program. The breakthrough came in discussions with FLS Energy in nearby Asheville. As a nonprofit organization, Kanuga could not take advantage of tax credits for solar energy and lacked the capital to purchase equipment for a large-scale solar thermal project. Brownie Newman, the director of project financing for FLS, helped to structure a transaction with a small group of investors who had tax obligations and could use the tax credits and pass the savings to Kanuga. In this arrangement, FLS owns and operates the equipment, and Kanuga buys the energy. "Our purchase of energy each month generates a bill equivalent to our bill for propane," Stan said. "Then the tax credit values flow to us." Kanuga received a bequest that enabled the center to pay an advance payment, or earnest money, of $50,000.

According to Stan, the project has a thirty-year lifespan for accounting purposes, but he expected the equipment to last longer. The solar energy system will heat the water used in the Kanuga Lake Inn's kitchen, laundry room, and sixty-two guest rooms, plus the ten other buildings on campus. With 131 solar panels installed on eleven buildings across the campus, Kanuga now heats approximately 1.5 million gallons of hot water per year through the energy of the sun. In the past, this water usage required burning more than 15,000 gallons of propane a year, which would cost Kanuga an estimated $1 million over the next thirty years. Through the transaction structured by Kanuga and FLS, the energy will cost about $300,000, resulting in a projected savings of $700,000 over the thirty-year life of the project.[8] The ultimate goal of financial arrangements like this is to allow nonprofits such as camps and conference centers to access solar energy at an affordable price. Other partners in this arrangement include Progress Energy Carolinas, which agreed to purchase renewable-energy credits, and two banks that provided both conventional and equity financing.

For other camps and conference centers interested in solar power, Stan listed the following step-by-step advice to maximize the success of the greening efforts:

1. *Walk before you run. Start small.* Install a small solar project at a kitchen or laundry facility, somewhere with a high usage of water, as a test site. "The small project will cause you to engage in financing and engineering," he said. "You'll prove to yourself and your board that solar works." Starting small also allows people time to get on board and get excited.

2. *Set more than financial goals.* Make visible the links of the solar project with the mission of your organization. Creating larger connections to the mission enhances the sustainability of the project.

3. *Empower your staff.* Give your board and staff leadership roles in the project. With multiple stakeholders playing leadership roles, the project becomes more viable.

4. *Expect to share your financing and technical schemes with other people.* "Think of yourself as a teaching hospital," Stan suggested. That perspective will give you energy when you are bogged down in logistics. The project then becomes about more than just your specific conference center.

5. *Don't give up on the financing.* For two years, Stan was told no to his requests for financing options for Kanuga's solar project. "If you have a vision, and it's mission-rooted, keep knocking on doors," he said. Others might call it serendipity, but the Holy Spirit is at work in these projects.

6. *Treat the greening initiative as discernment, not as a project.* "This is not about hope being the strategy," he said. "This is about being quiet enough to listen to opportunities that may arise. It's about discernment, which faith-based organizations get."

7. *Communicate with your board, your staff, and your community, because you never know who can help you.* Remain open to potential opportunities that may arise just by talking about the project with others.

Stan sees Kanuga as a change agent for the environment. "Kanuga is steeped in tradition," he said. "But we have modeled change by building on our early days of conservation." In their capacity as educators, the Kanuga staff members decided to put the holding tanks for the solar water system in full view because they wanted campers and guests to see and experience the system.

In collaboration with Sodexo, Kanuga's dining facilities started offering local foods whenever possible and buying from Mountain Food Products, a regional cooperative for local produce. "In the 1930s, staff grew our vegetables, so again, we are making historic connections to our past," Stan said. Kanuga also received a gift of $12,000 that enabled the purchase of 4,000 compact fluorescent bulbs, replacing every incandescent lightbulb at the camp and conference center. That green initiative has saved $1,000 every month off the electric bill. Next steps for environmental stewardship involve fundraising for the installation of a $2 million geothermal heating and cooling system for the Kanuga Inn, a building that uses inefficient electric heat.

Using Facilities as a Teaching Tool for Other Institutions Working with Youth

Founded in 1928, Kanuga treasures its 1,400-acre campus in the Appalachian mountains, known for high ecological diversity and high property values. Religious camps and conference centers have shared a status as "cash poor but land rich."[9] Indeed, the land assets provide one of the biggest resources for environmental education for youth ministry. But many denominations have felt pressure to view their land as a source of revenue in times of decreased donations and reduced income from investments. At Kanuga, however, the solar water-heating system has become a teaching tool in both financial and environmental stewardship, as the project models how similar institutions can save money and engage young people in environmental action.

Sandy Lynch, the vice president of property, spoke to me about Kanuga's facilities at a fast-clipped pace and with a rich North Carolina accent. Sandy did not sit still to show off the greening at Kanuga, but climbed into a staff vehicle for his narrated tour. With a thirty-five-year career at Kanuga, Sandy was a walking storyteller about this center, which he came to know as a teenager working there. He first drove me to the Kanuga Inn with its solar panels on the roof, and then we walked into the basement with its washers and dryers and the pipes that pump the hot water throughout the center.

As he talked, Sandy pointed out the holding tanks that contain 6,000 gallons of water, heated to a maximum of 160 degrees. "You put in 60-degree water and get out 120-degree water today," he said. Sandy took readings of the water temperature in the morning, noon, and night, keeping a log of the temperatures during the first year. His records showed that the solar water system produced on average the equivalent of 700 kilowatt hours per day for the last three months. Sandy shook his head and marveled, "That's the amount of energy we're making off this roof every day. Today, we'll have made the equivalent of 900 kilowatt hours." An average house uses 1,000–1,500 kilowatt hours per month. Thus, Kanuga is generating almost enough energy each day to supply the average home for one month.

The 131 solar panels were installed in February 2009 in about ten weeks of work. Sandy laughed when he looked at the panels on the roof of the Kanuga Inn and remembered the concerns of some staff and board members about the aesthetics of the panels. "Some people thought the panels would lie flat against the roof, but our roofs didn't have much slant," he recalled. "I say, if you're going to have these panels, jack 'em up. Show it off. Be proud of these panels." Jumping into a truck, Sandy continued the tour to show me the first solar panels at Camp Bob and the Mountain Trail Outdoor School and at his own home, right down the road. "This solar is the right thing to do," he said. "In this time and this economy, we all need to be sensible."

Since the installation of the solar panels, Sandy has given tours to western North Carolina institutions including Mars Hill College in Mars Hill, Christ School in Arden, and Deerfield Episcopal Retirement Community in Asheville. "People quickly see the financial benefits," he said. "In addition to going green, we are saving $35,000 a year. That amounts to $1 million over time—money we'll have available to fund something else." Sandy stressed that Kanuga was ready and willing to share the design and financing package with others.

As a teaching tool and model for financial stewardship, the green initiatives that help to educate youth at Kanuga have sparked changes in educational and religious institutions throughout the region. Following the Kanuga model, Montreat Conference Center, a Presbyterian center, has signed on with FLS Energy for a substantial solar project. Baptist-affiliated Mars Hill College is implementing another solar project with FLS that involves seventy-five solar thermal collectors to serve three college facilities and generate 3,000 gallons of hot water each day.[10]

The financial arrangement created by FLS Energy is called a power purchase agreement, and it allows an organization to purchase the solar energy without having to buy the equipment. Brownie Newman of FLS Energy said that a solar thermal system with a power purchase agreement can reduce net energy costs for organizations by 30–50 percent. As the owner of the equipment, FLS Energy can sell the renewable-energy certificates back to the utility companies. The result is a win-win situation that models environmental stewardship while saving money. According to Brownie, faith-affiliated institutions are perfect targets for large solar projects. When these projects become educational tools for youth, the impact goes beyond financial and environmental conservation.

Creation Spirituality as a Framework for Sunday School

Located about an hour from the forests of Kanuga, the face of Jubilee Community Church looks like an urban storefront, with a green awning atop its front door on Wall Street in downtown Asheville. Jubilee melds Christian mysticism with social and environmental justice, drawing on Matthew Fox's creation spirituality as a theological foundation. As Fox writes, "Creation is all things and us. It is us in relationship with all things."[11] To that end, the services incorporate ancient texts from both the Old and New Testaments, Buddhist texts for meditation, drumming and calling in the four directions, and a live band for music. The services follow the seasons—summer, fall, winter, and spring—and the corresponding paths of creation: via positiva, via negativa, via creativa, and via transformativa.

With its focus on creation, Jubilee attracts many artists, writers, and environmentalists, with an average of 700–800 worshippers each Sunday. When I visited, the sanctuary at Jubilee included a large open space with folding chairs arranged in a circle and four colorful banners for the vias, or pathways, on the walls. For via positiva, or summer, the banner featured bright red tomatoes, yellow daisies, a green tree, and a shining sun. During worship services, a round wooden table held offerings such as cut wildflowers, a bowl of water, a rock, and various icons. On one wall, a bright banner proclaimed, "Jubilee! Celebrating Creation." Creation spirituality focuses on original blessing, not original sin, but also acknowledges the darker sides of the human spirit. This theology draws from such mystical theologians as St. Francis of Assisi, St. Thomas Aquinas, and Julian of Norwich and is based in Christianity but also honors similar paths in Sufism, Buddhism, Taoism, and ancient Celtic religions.[12]

On a summer Sunday morning, children entered the Sunday school classroom for four- to eight-year-olds. Some children clung to the legs of their parents, while others waved goodbye, eager to see them go upstairs to the worship service. In the classroom, bright red letters spelled out "summer solstice" on a yellow background with pictures of flowers, the sun, and people (fig. 7.2). On another wall, a poster proclaimed the message: "I pledge allegiance to the earth, and the flora, the fauna, and the human life that supports one planet." A third wall provided the backdrop for a small altar with an image of the Virgin Mary, roses, and candles.

Figure 7.2 Jubilee Community Church integrates creation into its Sunday school curriculum. Photo by the author.

The children in this multi-age summer class sat around the table for a lesson in meditation led by guest teacher Maureen "Mo" Healy. In a quiet voice, Mo explained to the children the power of meditation to calm the mind. She demonstrated a breathing technique by asking the children to put one of their fingers over their right nostril and breathe in and out through their mouth. Then she asked them to close their left nostril, breathe in and breathe out through their mouth. An active four-year-old named Isabella exclaimed, "Breathing helps me when I'm hyper, and I'm always hyper!" The fidgety collective of children calmed when Mo told the children to close their eyes and imagine their favorite animal and the positive feelings they have for this animal. Mo continued the guided meditation: "Imagine being nice to your animal and take those good feelings, and imagine feeling that way to other people." The classroom was quiet for the two minutes of meditation, with only a few squirms and peeks.

Christian education for youth at Jubilee uses the four seasons as a framework for a green Sunday school curriculum. Currently, there are few Sunday school programs that give youth a year-round experience of growing in the Christian faith with an emphasis on creation. The Jubilee Community Nurture Program aims to fill that gap through its commitment to providing children a safe and loving environment where they can learn the stories and traditions of the Christian faith, recognize that they are loved unconditionally, trust that God is with them in every part of creation, and grow into stewards of the earth.[13]

This faith community held a series of workshops and focus groups to develop a framework for the curriculum, which includes rituals of celebration; universal sacred stories from the Bible, spiritual leaders like Buddha, other religions, and the earth community; experiential learning through meditation, the arts, games, and love of God; connecting with the community; and demonstrating compassion. To implement these pillars of the curriculum, the church hired Vicki Garlock, a pragmatic, straight-talking educator with a Ph.D. in psychology. As the nurture coordinator, Jubilee's version of a Sunday school coordinator, Vicki seeks to combine age-appropriate curricula with the diverse spiritual teachings at Jubilee. The church pays its Sunday school teachers $10 an hour, and Vicki designs appropriate lessons for each of the age levels.

Her goal is to transform the Jubilee curriculum into a published green Sunday school curriculum applicable to any denomination in the Christian faith. For Sunday school classes, most churches buy a published curriculum such as *Godly Play*.[14] At Jubilee, the teachers had tried this curriculum, which focuses on Bible stories, as well as *Living Values Activities*,[15] which emphasizes values like peace and respect but does not focus on any Bible stories. The church needed a curriculum that integrated multiple sources with an emphasis on creation.

To develop the curriculum, Vicki first drew on stories from the Bible. "The Bible is about people's relationship to land, the animals, food, preparation of food, the role of animal sacrifice," she said. "The Old Testament people were nomadic. An important part of under-standing the Bible is understanding the essence of that type of rela-tionship to the land." She gave the example of Jesus speaking to the Samaritan woman at the well, when Jesus says, "I am the living water." It's hard to understand that line as a modern kid if you get water by turning on the faucet, she acknowledged. Her lessons help children to understand how people in these ancient stories related to the natural environment and how the metaphors of the environment were important.

For the story that casts Jesus as the "salt of the earth," children need to understand the importance of salt as a preservative in a desert climate. "This is a grounding story for us because it is infused with the importance of nature," Vicki said. "Salt was a crucial spice for these people, and Jesus is saying he is the salt of the earth." Jesus used nature metaphors to relate to people 2,000 years ago, and Vicki's goal is to help children understand that relationship and the connection to nature today.

Mirroring the framework of the worship services, the seasons of creation help to structure the curriculum, drawing on holidays like the solstices and equinoxes. A source for those lessons is *Circle Round: Raising Children in the Goddess Traditions*,[16] which includes rituals, stories, recipes, and altars around Celtic goddess traditions focused on creation. In preparation for the summer solstice at Jubilee, young children talk about the sun and notice that the days have been getting longer, and older youth build altars honoring the sun. The lessons in the nurture program also integrate themes of nature from World Water Day and Earth Day, with activities including tree planting and creating jewelry from recycled materials. One goal is for youth to notice the creation around them; the days get longer or shorter, season after season, year after year.

By connecting youth to the ancient peoples and landscapes in the Bible, the Sunday school curriculum shows that we are not alone. "Children are part of something bigger," Vicki said. "They are a part of an age-old process where the sun rises, and the moon rises. Children will have hard times, and we can't predict when that will happen. But we can foster that innate connection to nature, which is one way you find your spiritual path." One goal of the green curriculum at Jubilee is to prepare children to discover the direction of their own spiritual journey in a faith community.

Christian Education for the "Thumb
Generation"

Christian educators today work with youth who may use Facebook and Twitter before and after Sunday school, church, and youth group meetings. Maria Roca is familiar with this reality, with a teenage daughter, a Ph.D. in communication, and a passion for faith and the environment. Given this background, she was determined to use video, a hip and engaging story line, and the power of parables to connect youth in congregations to environmental stewardship. She created a series of eco-spiritual parables that target religious youth groups from middle-school age to college. The characters in her parables are all teenagers who begin the story in their own world and get transported to the world of the parable. As part of a fellowship program with the religious environmental group GreenFaith, Maria is producing a total of six ten- to fifteen-minute videos under three subheadings: spirit, stewardship, and justice. The series will include two stories in each section, so youth groups will be able to show the entire series available on one DVD or focus on one section, such as justice.

The first parable, called *The Need*, highlights stewardship and features three teenage girls making plans to go shopping. The initial scene shows a girl with long black hair and glasses reaching into her closet, which is stuffed with clothes, and lamenting that she has "nothing" to wear. The next scene shows a second girl acting bored, proclaiming that she has "nothing" to do. The third girl in the video, the eco-heroine, brings her two friends on an eco-shopping excursion, a journey on which the girls shop in mainstream stores and a thrift store and try on ball gowns, shoes, and jewelry. But before they buy anything, they ask one question: Do I really need this?

That simple question transforms the experience into a shopping trip, not a buying trip. The eco-shopping trip becomes a vehicle for social interaction, not commercial engagement. With the help of the eco-heroine, the girls realize that they do not need most of the clothes they tried on. Just as important, the video shows the girls having fun, as they model in front of the mirror at the thrift shop, each decked out in a fancy ball gown. From the mall, the girls travel to a farmers' market, where they buy fresh fruits for a picnic by an urban lake. The short video concludes as the girls reflect during their picnic that, while they do not need all the clothes at the mall, they do need the beauty of their friendship.

As a professor of communications and interdisciplinary studies at Florida Gulf Coast University, Maria showed this video to one of her classes that focused on the Earth Charter. "The response was fabulous," she said. One month after the class, Maria was in Target and ran into one of the students in that class. "Anytime I'm shopping," the girl told Maria, "all I can hear in my head is those three girls asking if they need this item. And I keep coming back to the fact that I don't need this."

With an emphasis on spirit, the second story, *The Call*, focuses on the hyper-connection to technology, including iPods, cell phones, and computers, which can often block connections to the spirit. The third parable focuses on justice and features a girl looking at all her

possessions and seeing beyond the products to the people who produced the items: a child laborer in the Dominican Republic, an immigrant worker picking fruit in the United States. Maria is working
with an Iranian videographer, Farshad Aminian, to produce the six
vignettes. She is writing a study guide to accompany the ninety-min-
utes of video, which she will distribute through the religious environmental organization GreenFaith.

Each vignette closes with quotations from a diversity of religious
texts—Christian, Jewish, Muslim, Buddhist—that illustrate the lesson of the eco-spiritual parable. During the eco-shopping parable, for
example, one of the ending quotations is from Ephesians 5:15: "Be
careful there how you live, not as unwise people, but as wise." The
actors in the videos are real teens, including Maria's daughter Alissa
and a former student who plays the male spirit guide in *The Call*. As
a college professor, Maria also hopes to target campus ministries in the
distribution of the DVD.

The production of these parables has made a dramatic impact on
many aspects of Maria's own life, including her consumer behaviors
and her classes. "I stopped shopping when I made a commitment to
this project," she said. "I now shop in my closet." Maria admitted that
she has a deep love of shoes. "I was in New York, and I saw this pair
of shoes," she recounted. "I loved them. What is the cultural text that
is so deep in me that I had a hard time not buying the shoes?" The
video that focuses on spirit impacted the questions she asked of her
students in classes. She began integrating contemplative practices
into her Earth Charter class: guided meditation, walking meditation,
deep listening, free writing, and partner reflection. She has used resources from the Center for Contemplative Mind in Society, such as a
visual called "The Tree of Contemplative Practices," which depicts a
variety of practices.[17]

Maria believes that faith communities have a strong role to play
in shaping the behaviors of youth through education. "I've become
so much more aware of the environmental themes in the gospels,"
she said. "Even Jesus tells the apostles of the need to rest. We can't
continue at this current pace." With these parables, Maria is drawing on her knowledge of communication theory about how people

learn. Narrative theory tells us that, if you can see yourself in one of the roles in a narrative, you can learn through stories. Jesus taught in parables, and these stories are designed as parables in which young people can see themselves in the story, making decisions that protect God's earth.

Educating Youth as a Ministry: Lessons Learned

To remain relevant, Christian education must engage young people in issues that matter to their lives and their communities. Youth ministry on the hiking trails of Kanuga Conferences, in the Sunday school classes at Jubilee, and in Maria Roca's eco-parables reveals important practices for connecting faith and environment in our congregations.

Use land owned by religious institutions to engage youth in the outdoors.

Many of today's youth suffer from what Richard Louv calls "nature deficit disorder," a significant lack of time spent in unstructured play outdoors. Research has shown the importance of time outside to the physical, emotional, and cognitive development of children. As churches approach Christian ministry, they can use land owned by their denominations as an ideal context for addressing this need and building an environmental ethic grounded in faith. Young people today hear about environmental destruction in both school and the media. Camps and conference centers in natural settings offer space for experiential education to connect young people to ecological resources and a spiritual home.

Work to make educational facilities reflect environmental values through creative approaches to financing.

Christian education that integrates the environment becomes stronger if the facilities reflect the same environmental values as the programming.

The buildings can provide models of sustainable environmental design. The leadership at Kanuga has envisioned these green initiatives as a process of discernment, listening to God's will for its future as an institution. While many nonprofits may want solar energy in their buildings, they may lack the capital to invest in the equipment up front. Religious institutions also might not benefit from tax credits due to their nonprofit status. But creative financing approaches can be tapped, such as the power purchase agreement developed by FLS Energy for Kanuga Conferences, which installed one of the largest solar water-heating systems in the Southeast. This arrangement allowed Kanuga to purchase the renewable energy it generates without a direct purchase of the equipment.

Use facilities as a teaching tool for other institutions working with youth.

Religious camps and conference centers that reflect environmental values serve as models, as teaching tools, to other religious institutions that educate youth. Stan Hubbard, the president of Kanuga Conferences, sees the role of Kanuga as a "teaching hospital," a role that involved sharing information on its solar water-heating system with other institutions. By sharing information about the design and the financial arrangement, Kanuga has influenced several large religious educational institutions to invest in similar solar systems.

Integrate creation into Sunday school classes.

Connecting creation to Sunday school classes may take different forms, depending on the curriculum and teachers at a church. For Jubilee, the seasons of creation formed a framework to connect youth to the natural world around them. This connection involved teaching strategies as diverse as music, biblical verses, crafts, and outdoor activities, each geared to specific age groups. At this church, the congregation decided to invest resources in hiring a Sunday school coordinator to green the curriculum. Another option might be working with Sunday school teachers to brainstorm opportunities to infuse environmental activities and priorities into the classes. Many classes across the country have engaged high-school students, for example, in an energy audit of their church.[18] Youth often can take leadership roles in creating an environmental angle for their Sunday school or youth group.

> *Diversify educational strategies to include relevant media and*
> *technology that promote environmental stewardship for youth.*

The traditional hard-copy curriculum packet cannot stand alone as the sole strategy to engage youth in Christian education for the environment. A diversity of methods is needed to reach those with diverse learning styles, including kinesthetic learners who need to move outdoors and visual learners who need images and pictures. Addressing different learning styles through media and technology in Christian education is one strategy to reach youth, who may have used Facebook to chat with a friend on the way to church. The DVD developed by Maria Roca at Florida Gulf Coast University uses the power of parables and narrative theory to show teens examples of responsible behavior connected to their faith and the environment.

On Reflection

Church camp is in my blood. The lineage starts with my grandfather, the Reverend Cecil B. Jones, an Episcopal priest who helped to build Camp Bratton-Green in the Mississippi pinelands. On my bookshelf at home is a framed black-and-white picture of my grandfather in a striped tie and dress shirt as he canoes with my mother and uncle, young children who are "fishing" with a stick in the lake at Camp Bratton-Green. They spent every summer of their youth there, where my grandfather was the camp director. My uncle later became a priest and assumed the role of camp director during the summers.

Visiting Camp Bratton-Green for family reunions, I heard story after story about a faith lived out in this special place, with outdoor worship services held on the shore of the lake. As a high-school student, I worked as a counselor at Camp Beckwith, located on Weeks

Bay near Fairhope, Alabama. We canoed in the bay, hiked in the woods, and spent hours singing, praying, and helping children to discover this outdoor space as a spiritual home.

For many, Christian camping programs are a luxury, but my interviews with Christian educators reinforced my belief that we can create immersion experiences in our Sunday schools and youth groups as well. Indeed, given the opportunity, young people will generate ideas for addressing environmental issues and engaging with the outdoors from their church home. Our churches can create venues for youth to have a collective experience with the environment that pulls them outside their everyday existence and empowers them in a positive way.

While conducting energy audits of their church or installing solar panels at camp, youth engaged in the church are eager for relevant experiences that steward God's earth. When I was a camp counselor, I felt that church was mine at Camp Beckwith, different from the building where I went to worship with my parents each week. And in the end, that realization was part of writing my own spiritual history.

8

Bearing Witness

Engaging People of Faith in Environmental Advocacy

You are my witnesses, says the Lord, and my servant whom I have chosen, so that you may know and believe me and understand that I am he. Before me no god was formed, nor shall there be any after me.

—Isaiah 43:10 (NRSV)

A thousand acts of Christian kindness can be wiped away by a single act of Congress.

—LeeAnne Beres, executive director,
Earth Ministry

The parish hall of University Presbyterian Church in Seattle, Washington was ready for a typical church function scheduled for the noon hour—circular tables with white cloths, name tags for participants, pitchers of iced tea, a buffet lunch, and the hum of social chitchat. But this was not the usual church luncheon; advocacy around climate change was the focus of this gathering of Methodists, Presbyterians, Catholics, Lutherans, Mennonites, United Church of Christ members, and evangelicals. Fifty faith leaders from these diverse traditions were assembled in Seattle for this event, "What Every Pastor Needs to Know about Climate Change."

To begin the program, LeeAnne Beres, the executive director of Earth Ministry, a religious environmental organization based in

Seattle, posed a question to the group: "Why should Christians care about creation?" Hands shot up across the room, and the responses included our responsibility to protect creation for our children and our call to care for the poor. LeeAnne cited a study that found that 80 percent of people feel they have their strongest connection to God in the natural world. By the end of the luncheon, each faith leader had signed the Call to Care, a letter to members of the U.S. Congress asking for the protection of species imperiled by climate change.[1]

"A thousand acts of Christian kindness can be wiped away by a single act of Congress," said LeeAnne. This powerful sound bite reflects the importance of our prophetic voice in the care of God's creation. As Christians, we hear the call to proclaim the good news. When we bear witness to God's love, we move from the safety of our churches to the public arena, to congressional offices and city council meetings.

Churches involved with Earth Ministry are bringing their faith and moral voice to bear witness for the environment, protecting the Pacific Northwest and enhancing the relevance of Christianity in a region described as the most unchurched area of the nation.[2] Earth Ministry has become a leader for churches across the country that want to prepare Christians to influence the environmental agenda in a political landscape and incorporate progressive faith values into civic life.[3] As LeeAnne said, being active followers of Christ should involve lobbying legislators, speaking at rallies, and engaging in environmental advocacy on behalf of all of God's creation (fig. 8.1).

When she speaks with congregations, LeeAnne uses a metaphor of a three-legged stool to describe the religious environmental movement.[4] The first leg is the individual, reflecting our personal connection with faith and the environment. As individual Christians, we are called to live lightly on the earth and to love our neighbors as ourselves. This manifests in everyday choices about how we eat, drive, use energy and water, and other aspects of daily life. The second leg of the stool is the community. Once people have made the connection between their faith and caring for the earth, they are naturally drawn to others who share those values; in the religious

Figure 8.1   Congregations affiliated with Earth Ministry
express their care of creation through environmental advocacy.
Photo by Earth Ministry.

community, this often translates into reflecting that faith at the congregational level. Earth Ministry works with churches through its
Greening Congregations program in four areas: worship and education; facilities and institutional life; community outreach; and de-
nominational, ecumenical, and interfaith efforts.[5] The third leg of
the stool is advocacy and systemic change. "We as people of faith have
a right and responsibility to speak up and ensure our voices are heard
in public policy," LeeAnne told me. Earth Ministry approaches advocacy through specific values that address the reasons that Christians
should care about creation, including sustainability, stewardship, justice, and spirituality.

With a staff of only four people, Earth Ministry incorporates
these shared values in legislative campaigns like the Local Farms–
Healthy Kids initiative and the Green Jobs initiative, both of which
passed the Washington state legislature in the 2008 session, and in
testimony before the EPA at hearings on the impact of climate
change.[6] Earth Ministry staff model this advocacy, writing opinion
pieces on climate change for the *Seattle Times* and lobbying legislators

in Olympia, the state capital, and in Washington, DC.[7] The work of churches in Earth Ministry reveals how Christians learn to articulate their faith story and its mandate for environmental stewardship.

This chapter shows how an environmental lens has transformed the ministry of bearing witness and increased the relevance of churches in a region more known for secular environmental values. Through this prophetic side of ministry, Earth Ministry and its member churches have become strong players in shaping legislation that affects the health of God's people and places. In this chapter, we meet advocates such as Earth Ministry's Jessie Dye, a former attorney who now trains parishioners in environmental advocacy, and Pastor Carol Jensen, who views the baptismal covenant as a call for both grace and activism. The lessons include working with diverse denominations in the political process, advocating for specific pieces of legislation, clarifying values and training church members in advocacy, and taking steps toward advocacy by the greening of congregations.

Presbyterians and Evangelicals: Bringing the
Religious Voice to the Political Process

"You can turn on Fox News and see critiques regarding climate change or the environment, but now they have to criticize both evangelicals and the environmentalists who are supporting the same issues," said the Reverend Richard Cizik, a former vice president of governmental affairs with the National Association of Evangelicals. In 2008, *Time* magazine named him one of the hundred most influential people in the world. Earth Ministry invited Rev. Cizik to Seattle to add his evangelical message of creation care to the campaign entitled "Irreplaceable: A Faith Response to Wildlife in a Warming World." This advocacy campaign included a traveling art exhibit featuring wildlife threatened by climate change. During the exhibit's run in Seattle, Earth Ministry partnered with two other religious environmental groups, the Noah Alliance and Restoring Eden, to organize the pastors' lunch on climate change and then an evening panel at the Burke Museum of Natural History and Culture on the campus of the University of Washington.

At the evening event, a crowd of about 200 people snacked on local cheeses, breads, fruits, and teas before viewing the museum's colorful, bold photographs of wildlife. The panel for the event at the museum featured speakers from diverse faith backgrounds, including Rev. Cizik; Bishop Chris Boerger of the Northwest Washington Synod of the Evangelical Lutheran Church in America (ELCA); the Reverend Lisa Domke, a Presbyterian minister; and Yolanda Quiroga, the youth and environmental minister of St. Mary's Catholic Church. LeeAnne began the evening with a succinct statement of her organization's mission: "At Earth Ministry, we work with individuals, congregations, and communities to engage people of faith in environmental stewardship." She asked each speaker to talk about how his or her faith tradition engages people of faith in creation care and halting climate change.

With a clerical collar and a cross around his neck, Bishop Boerger reminded the audience that the earth and all that exists were created by God. "In Genesis 2, humans were told to till and to keep the earth. Another translation is to serve and protect," he said. The bishop described humans as co-creators with God, here not to subdue the earth, but to protect it. Indeed, he called the care of the earth "a profoundly spiritual matter."

A minister and a mother, Rev. Domke then recalled her own call to faith in the arena of public policy. "I stopped being able to keep my faith in the private realm," she said. She believes that some churches spend time focused on maintaining institutions, acting as if this world, here and now, doesn't matter because we are going to heaven. "Jesus gives us permission to become concerned with what is going on now," she said, emphasizing that Jesus is a role model for engaging policy makers on important issues of the day. Rev. Domke stressed that the kingdom of God is not coming in some future time, but even now is here among us, within us. "It's not pie in the sky in the by and by," she said. "It's now."

Rev. Cizik followed her comments with his own story of growing up on a farm in eastern Washington but then leaving his home state behind. He worked from 1980 to 2008 for the National Association of Evangelicals but admitted that, until 2002, he had given the issue of the environment "about one hour of thought." Then, he was invited by evangelical leader Jim Ball to attend a conference on the science of climate change at Oxford University in England. That conference resulted in what Rev. Cizik called a "conversion" experience, a "repentance for living the wrong way for a long time." The congruence and consistency of the messages from the diverse faith leaders on the panel pointed to the power of aligning political will, values, and behavior in the face of climate change.

Targeting Specific Legislation with Faith and Environmental Partners

The next morning, Jessie Dye, an attorney turned religious environmental activist, drove her weathered Subaru to a planning meeting for Faith Advocacy Day. As program and outreach director for Earth Ministry, Jessie works hand in hand with LeeAnne Beres to boost the efforts of congregations in environmental advocacy. With an engaging and straightforward manner, Jessie seemed to stay focused on the task in front of her while maintaining a sense of humor. As we climbed into her car, she apologized for the dog hairs on the seats. "I can't get a new car until my second child graduates from college, and he's a freshman now," she said with a smile of resignation. In leaving her career as an attorney specializing in conflict resolution, Jessie took a two-thirds pay cut to work for Earth Ministry.

She talked quickly, stringing together stories of advocacy as she drove from the Earth Ministry offices, located on the third floor of Trinity United Methodist Church, to a meeting across town. Jessie grew up in the Catholic Church and uses that religious foundation in her work with Earth Ministry. "My two big areas of focus are outreach and advocacy," she began. "What we accomplished at the pastors' lunch was true outreach, with evangelical pastors in the room, along with mainline Protestant ministers," she said. Earth

Ministry recruited clergy from twenty-five different congregations to the lunch, a showing that Jessie described as "phenomenal."

Each year, Earth Ministry partners with the environmental community to plan Environmental Lobby Day and with religious organizations to plan Faith Advocacy Day for the state of Washington. On both days, individuals and organizations travel to the state capital to receive training in advocacy and to lobby legislators on priority bills. Environmental Lobby Day has been an annual event in Olympia for ten years, and in planning the event, Earth Ministry collaborates with the top twenty-five environmental groups in the state, including Climate Solutions, the Sierra Club, the Audubon Society, and the Washington Environmental Council. Earth Ministry was the first religious organization to join this coalition in 2006, in large part because of LeeAnne's leadership, background in fisheries biology, and experience working with environmental groups. In 2009, there were 500 people involved in Environmental Lobby Day, and Earth Ministry was responsible for recruiting 20 percent of them. "Once you make the path from your house to the state legislature, it's easy to do it again," Jessie said.

Each year, the executive directors of the environmental groups meet to establish four legislative priorities.[8] These "environmental priorities," the targets for legislative advocacy during the year, focus on the health of the land, air, and water, and hence on the health of the people of the state. The record of legislative success speaks to the power of this coalition. In 2008, all four bills were passed: Climate Action and Green Jobs; Local Farms–Healthy Kids; Evergreen Cities; and Local Solutions to Global Warming.

In 2009, the priorities were bills focused on climate change, energy efficiency, transit-oriented communities, and clean water. Half of the bills passed in the state legislature, which LeeAnne called a success given the reality of the state budget deficit. The coalition uses a structured process to identify the year's four legislative priorities. Jessie sits on the team of organizers for the Environmental Priorities Coalition and described the need for a long-term strategy to convince the other groups to support each initiative. In the fall, the executive directors of all the organizations gather for "intense horse-trading." But once those four priorities are chosen, all the groups get on board.

Earth Ministry has an advantage in this process, she said, as the organization is not focused on single issues or ecosystems, such as salmon, health, or rivers. "We're not an issues group. We are a constituency group," she said. "We are not there every year for trees or salmon. We are there for the faith community." Throughout the year, Jessie trains people of faith to identify why they should care and what they can do to help pass the legislation.

Jessie reiterated the image of the three legs of the stool in regard to religious environmentalism: individual action, congregational commitments, and public policy. "I'm going to teach you how to engage in the political process," she said. "We have already established why people of faith should care about the earth. We are tenants of the creation. We are here to care for the poor, who are most affected by climate change and other environmental devastation." As Jessie spoke, she pulled up to the Denny Park Lutheran Church, home of the Lutheran Public Policy Office, the advocacy organization for the three ELCA synods in the state. At this office, seven other members of the planning committee gathered, representing the Washington Association of Churches, the Church Council of Greater Seattle, the United Methodist Church, the United Church of Christ, and the ELCA.

One goal for the organizers of Faith Advocacy Day was to broaden the interdenominational representation. The facilitator, the Reverend Paul Benz from the state's Lutheran Public Policy Office, called the meeting to order and asked for volunteers to recruit people for the day of lobbying in Olympia. "Who can contact the Presbyterians?" he started. "What about Disciples of Christ? the Quakers? the Unitarians? the Baptists? the AME church?" Everyone volunteered for different denominations or else volunteered someone they knew. The organizers called out the names of denominations, as if they were reading items off a grocery list. When committee members volunteered to target a denomination, Paul would ask them to commit to a number. How many people do you think you can turn out from the Methodists? The planning group set a goal of 350 participants for the entire event, which would involve registration, worship, briefing, an issues workshop, lunch, and lobbying.

Afterward, Jessie jumped back in the car, eager to recap the meeting with me. She reiterated her advocacy goal of passing the environmental priorities. She ticked off the names of denominations that will help to focus her own training efforts in congregations. To broaden its reach, in 2008, Earth Ministry added interfaith outreach to its advocacy efforts with the start of Washington Interfaith Power & Light.[9] This initiative involves outreach to Jewish, Muslim, and Buddhist groups, for example, in addition to Christian congregations.

Values and Spaces to Involve Churches in
Advocacy

As she joined LeeAnne in a conference room to talk about Earth Ministry's training sessions in environmental advocacy, Jessie whispered to me, like an undercover agent, "Would you like a Fresca?" She laughed about the perceived environmental "sin" of drinking a soda, with its packaging and artificial sweetener. "That's the problem with the environmental movement," she said. "We're perceived as judgmental. In the end, we are all human. Our Earth Ministry blog is about sharing our struggles." Each staff member contributes to the blog and shares thoughts about practices as diverse as Lenten disciplines of reducing water consumption, using public transportation, or lobbying the legislature. One of Jessie's past blog entries revealed her personal attempts to eat more sustainably, and her writing portrayed her as a human advocate for God's earth.

Connecting Environmental Advocacy to Values of Faith   To train people of faith in advocacy, Earth Ministry believes that church members must be able to articulate the values that connect faith to care of creation. As LeeAnne explained, this is a faith-based advocacy program, not simply another take on secular activism. "We believe we connect to the earth through God," she said.

She described the four key values that form the foundation of the trainings:

1. Sustainability. We must meet the needs of the present without compromising the ability of future generations to meet their needs. Sustainability means seeing ourselves and our neighbors as children of God.

2. Stewardship. We are tenants of creation for future generations and all species. Creation is good and sacred, because God created all of the earth and us. Thus, we are called by our love for God's works to protect them.

3. Justice. We are called to change structural systems that cause poverty, injustice, and environmental damage. We must create a society with laws and policies that allow the needs of all of earth's inhabitants to be met.

4. Spirituality. Many people have their most profound spiritual experiences in nature. Creation inspires us and calls us to care, and God is our inspiration to care for this earth.

In their Advocacy for All Creation workshops, LeeAnne and Jessie start by asking, "Why do people of faith care for the earth?" The answers look back to these core values. The next questions they frame are, "What is the response of people of faith? What are we going to do?" The answers lie in the three-legged stool, with its emphasis on individual action, congregational initiative, and political advocacy. In the advocacy workshops, the facilitators often start with an abbreviated version of Government 101. Most of the work done by Earth Ministry is in the state legislature, although it has a national presence in its work with the National Council of Churches and Interfaith Power & Light on key environmental bills in Congress.

LeeAnne showed me the handout for the workshop, subtitled "A Faithful Citizen's Guide to Participating in a Democracy."[10] Their first question, "Why do people of faith care about creation?" prompts workshop participants to write down the four values of sustainability, stewardship, justice, and spirituality as the most important reasons to advocate for creation when they talk to their elected officials. The second section, the Government 101 review, asks people of faith to list the three branches of government—legislative, judicial, and executive. The workshop also reminds participants of the three levels of government—federal, state, and local—and their respective legislative bodies, the U.S. Congress, the state legislature, and the city council. This introduction sets the stage for building comfort in interactions with the government and building concrete skills to influence policy.

Environmental Advocacy: As Easy as Ordering Pizza   Jessie has developed an analogy that advocacy for God's creation is "as easy as ordering pizza." The last section of the training focuses on how to influence elected officials to protect God's earth. Washington State has a hotline, a toll-free number to handle calls from voters about legislation. When a citizen calls that number, the operator asks for the caller's name and address and will identify his or her representatives and senators. Callers then may tell the operator what bills they support, and why.

In the advocacy workshop, Jessie and LeeAnne explain that the "why" for supporting the bills involves values of faith. As the handouts detail, "Be sure to identify yourself as a person of faith by your denomination and specific church. That doesn't mean you are speaking on behalf of your church or denomination, but it makes it clear you are representing the moral voice for protecting God's gift of creation, which can't speak for itself." The metaphor of ordering pizza begins with knowing both what you want and the phone number for the pizza delivery place. Unlike ordering pizza, however, you don't need to pay, as this service is free.

Having identified the year's environmental priorities, Earth Ministry gives participants four concrete bills they can support that are backed by their faith values. In the training, parishioners practice articulating faith values in support of specific bills. As Jessie said, "I believe that caring for God's creation is my responsibility as a Catholic, so I support the bill that will eliminate toxic chemicals from plastic baby bottles."

The trainings always incorporate hands-on, experiential learning about faith and advocacy; LeeAnne and Jessie distribute cardboard phones, similar to those that pizzerias provide, imprinted with the Washington state legislature's toll-free number. They ask people to pull out their cell phones, then and there, and program the Washington legislative hotline into their phones. Then, with no procrastination or doubts, two people from the class are asked to make calls and speak to the hotline operator. "When they hang up, people actually burst into applause," LeeAnne said. "It's empowering." Many people have never called their legislators; Jessie tells them that calling the governor is like adding double pepperoni to your pizza order. The workshop also walks people through the process of talking directly with elected officials. As Jessie said, "It takes seven contacts to any legislator to elevate an issue to the point where you have their attention."

LeeAnne believes that advocacy is what it means to be a follower of Christ. As Christians, we are taught to love our neighbors as ourselves. We house the homeless, feed the poor. For the environment, we may recycle, compost, and use compact fluorescent lights (CFLs). To her, loving our neighbor as ourselves means loving plants, animals, and ecosystems, in addition to our human brothers and sisters. But she believes we cannot stop there. Her personal witness to Christ calls her to advocacy. "Jesus was out there challenging the status quo," she said. "He healed on the Sabbath. That was a political act." She believes in her responsibility to speak up and offer a prophetic witness, which moves her to testify to the state legislature.

LeeAnne spoke about her own religious journey when she found her church home in the United Church of Christ. "I was raised in a nonreligious household," she said. "I became a Christian because of this work. It was never about personal salvation for me or sitting in church services since childhood. The prophetic voice was what drew me in."

She spoke about a personal desire to reclaim what it means to be Christian in the United States. She tires of people, especially in the secular Northwest, thinking that Christians are "war-loving, consumer-loving people." In her previous job, LeeAnne worked as associate director for Save Our Wild Salmon in Washington. "When I left to work for Earth Ministry, a colleague of mine in the environmental community told me, 'I can't believe you are one of them.'" The "them" in this case was Christians. For her, the work has become a personal passion to identify Christians as people who are not judgmental of others and who work for the common good of all people and the planet.

With her connections in the secular environmental movement, LeeAnne brought Earth Ministry into the fold of the Environmental Priorities Coalition. "The environmentalists now see that we can deliver," Jessie said. For the Seattle Green Festival in 2008, the city had two spots for speakers: one for the mayor and one for LeeAnne from Earth Ministry. As Earth Ministry has demonstrated its political will, environmental and government groups want to align themselves with this organized constituency from the faith community.

Their training workshops end with seven tips for communicating as people of faith with elected officials:

1. Identify yourself as a person of faith by denomination or church or as a member of Earth Ministry.
2. Try to find something good your elected official has done recently and thank him or her for it.
3. Pick one or, at most, two issues to focus on at a time.
4. Be clear about what you are asking the elected official to do.
5. Speak from the heart.
6. Don't get sidetracked by rhetoric.
7. Remember that your elected officials work for you.

LeeAnne also preaches sermons linking advocacy to biblical texts, such as a sermon she gave on faith and advocacy to the First Congregational Church in Walla Walla, Washington. The gospel for that day was Luke 5:1–11, when the disciples left their nets, boats, friends, and family to follow Jesus. LeeAnne's sermon raised the question of how many of us would be ready to respond to God's call to service today. "I'd probably be hemming and hawing on the shores of the lake, trying to negotiate some kind of telecommuting discipleship," she said.[11]

Her sermon suggests that the call to discipleship might not be about packing our bags but rather leaving our own comfort zones and our apathy—and, in the case of creation care, engaging our own voices in community action and advocacy. It also reminds people of faith of the words of Micah: "What does the Lord require of you? To do justice, love kindness, and walk humbly with your God." As Christians, LeeAnne writes, we must work to change social systems, practices, and attitudes that lead to injustice. Justice can be achieved only through getting involved in our communities and our government. "If a single decision by a city council or the Washington state legislature can either enhance or undo thousands of individual acts of Christian caring, should we not try to influence such decisions?"[12] As Isaiah 58:1 compels us, "Shout out, do not hold back! Lift up your voice like a trumpet!" Engaging in policy advocacy, LeeAnne said, is a necessary next step in our commitment to achieving Jesus' vision of a just and loving society.

Steps toward Advocacy by Greening Congregations

A large part of Earth Ministry's work is its Greening Congregations program, which supports congregations in cultivating creation care within their houses of worship and in moving toward advocacy. A major resource is its *Greening Congregations Handbook*, which includes a wealth of information and direction for churches taking the first steps toward greening.[13] The text presents six dimensions of greening—mission statements, worship, education, institutional life, community outreach, and broader religious outreach—with examples of greening efforts in each area.

The process of greening a congregation often starts with the creation of a green team or a creation care task force. Indeed, a survey by Cassandra Carmichael, Laurel Kearns, and Rebecca Gould found that, at most churches, a small group of committed people lead the efforts to integrate environmental issues into the life of the church.[14] But Earth Ministry encourages churches to seek institutional support from the church council or vestry so as to avoid isolated groups of people working on greening efforts. At an annual St. Francis event, Earth Ministry honors the congregations that have completed the greening process by presenting them with a banner to hang in their sanctuary. Integrating earth care throughout the life of a congregation results in more effective and strategic advocacy. The stories below reflect the different paths of two congregations in bearing witness for education, worship, and advocacy.

Raspberries, Blackberries, and Baptism   The garden at Trinity United Methodist Church, the home of the Earth Ministry office, boasted an abundance of raspberries, blackberries, parsley, and basil in July. The small and inviting church garden featured painted wooden signs that read, for example, "Gardenkeeper June," the name of the parishioner who tended that tiny plot. As the sun crept through clouds on this July day, the Reverend Rich Lang sat with me by the garden and described how his church took steps to green the congregation and promote advocacy for the earth. An engaging man with a sharp wit and self-deprecating sense of humor, Rev. Lang served as the pastor at Trinity United Methodist Church and as a board member of Earth Ministry. The church started a soup kitchen and wanted the organic garden as a resource for the food pantry as well as for the community. Now, different teams weed discrete plots, and each team decides what to plant.

The more theology he read, the more Rev. Lang realized that we were created with a purpose to partner with God in care of creation. He described his belief in the biblical concept of the jubilee—the recycling of wealth, of life. With a jubilee, the land gets rested, the slaves get freed, the rich have to return their wealth, and the poor get a slice of the pie. He aimed for Trinity United Methodist Church to function as a jubilee church with environmental ministry as a part of that vision. Earth Ministry helped to jump-start the environmental work at Trinity, providing resources that focused on food, car-free Sundays, educational modules, special events, advocacy, and the *Greening Congregations Handbook.*[15]

At the congregational level, Rev. Lang emphasized the need to start small. Five years ago, the church got rid of Styrofoam. After that step, the members started serving fair-trade coffee and began the pesticide-free garden. The church integrated greening into the infrastructure of the building in partnership with Seattle Public Utilities, which promoted replacing all incandescent lightbulbs with CFLs. Faced with unsustainable heating bills, the church also installed a new $60,000 natural-gas boiler system. "A wise church will understand that you go at this greening with small steps, and your faith will lead you to bigger steps," he said. "Then, you will look back and see you have changed the mindset of the entire congregation."

For Rev. Lang, baptism is an entry into a new creation. The Eucharist is a living sign that we give bread away. We feed people as a political act. If churches can begin with a commitment that no one who shares fellowship will be alone or homeless, that will revolutionize the church, he said. He also maintained that his church must integrate the environment into its ministry to stay relevant to younger parishioners, who want their church life to reflect their environmental values and, ultimately, want to influence public policy.

Soup Kitchens, Sanctuaries, and the Legislature   Across town in the Phinney Ridge area of Seattle, parishioners at St. John United Lutheran Church described their small, red-brick building as a church whose soup kitchen has the best view of Puget Sound. And it did: from the windows of the church basement, the church gardens in the foreground were set off by the water, boats, and the surrounding peaks of the Olympic mountains as a backdrop. Advocacy, worship, and greening played supporting roles at St. John United Lutheran Church.

In the summer, to diminish paper usage, the ushers at St. John United distributed a set bulletin for the service, with a one-page insert for that week's hymns and readings. The decision highlighted the need to conserve paper products as a concrete act of stewardship. As the service started, the congregation sang hymn 879, "For the beauty of the Earth, for the beauty of the skies," a reminder of the power of hymns to connect Christians to place and, more broadly, to God's earth.

Pastor Carol Jensen used the parable of the mustard seed to describe the power of God to transform the little things we do into big things. She highlighted the soup kitchen in the church, started twenty-five years ago and now going strong with the help of the organic church garden. From a small start, the church had served a half million meals. Small actions can grow bigger than anyone could have seen or imagined, she said.

After the service, in the basement with the beautiful view, two gray-haired women with perfect posture served tea and coffee from a silver tea service. Pastor Carol sat down with several women from the church, including Kris Freeman, an Earth Ministry member who grew up Presbyterian but described herself as "more agnostic than Lutheran." She turned to look me in the eye and said, "Pastor Carol knows this about me; it's okay." Kris described the important role of the church in civil rights as analogous to its growing importance in the environmental movement. Working in the church, for her, was a way to develop social consensus for environmental change. Kris drew a strong connection between the hope of her faith and her momentum around environmental work. "I was very depressed about the state of the planet," she said. "But now I have more hope that it is possible to make a small difference."

Pastor Carol spoke candidly about the strategic environmental emphasis of the church. "For the church to have any relevance to people in this Phinney Ridge/Ballard area, we need to have environmental relevance," she said. "The new people who come to our church come because the environment is part of our identity." Then she posed a critical question: "In the most secular city in the country, how do you sustain a church?" Indeed, there is a large Lutheran church right down the street. "We would be dead now without this environmental focus," she admitted, noting that the old categories of church membership are less important than in the past, while practicing our faith is more important. At St. John United, parishioners talk about the "upstairs" church with the sanctuary and the "downstairs" church with the homeless shelter and the garden, both critical components of the ministry.

An Earth Care Season to Integrate Creation into Education, Worship, and Advocacy   Pastor Carol believes in bringing the natural world— seeds, soils, rocks, and water—into the sanctuary. One year, she even brought a cherry tree into the church in a wheelbarrow. Bringing elements of God's earth into the church was part of Earth Care Season, a liturgical season of creation developed by Pastor Carol and members of the congregation for the three Sundays after Easter. The worship services for these three Sundays followed the celebration of the resurrection of Christ, a sign of redemption for God's whole creation, including wildlife, the seas, and the skies. The church started the season with Celebrate Planet Earth and the Land Sunday, which concluded with a procession and blessing by the entire congregation of the church garden. The next Sunday, the congregation focused on Save the Oceans and Puget Sound, which they can see from the church grounds. The concluding service featured the theme of Caring for This Place—our church, homes, and neighborhoods.

To integrate creation care into educational programming, the middle-school Sunday school class studied and presented ways that the church impacts the environment; the students did research on utility costs, water usage, number of CFLs, and how to improve energy efficiency. The culminating event for the season was an Earth Care Fair after the worship service on the last Sunday, with tables from community groups, opportunities for advocacy, music, and children's activities. For each liturgy, the worship arts committee created fabric collages featuring the natural elements, such as Puget Sound, that were the focus of that Sunday.

Pastor Carol makes the connection among education, worship, and advocacy, as she sees direct links among these aspects of church life. She serves as chair of the Lutheran Public Policy Office's advisory council. In 2008, her congregation partnered with Earth Ministry in the passage of the Local Farms–Healthy Kids act in the state legislature. Parishioners mobilized letters of support and attended Faith Lobbying Day in Olympia. On the local level, members of the congregation used the time after church to sign postcards to the Seattle City Council supporting a twenty-cent tax on plastic bags in grocery stores, as part of an effort to persuade the city's residents to opt for reusable canvas bags. Coffee hour often included a table with information about an issue, with opportunities to sign up for support.

To model advocacy to the congregation, Pastor Carol has represented clergy for Earth Ministry through such means as testifying before the governor's climate action team. She also represented her church at the EPA hearings in May 2009 on the impact of global warming on public health (fig. 8.2). Pastor Carol brought the discussion back to the biblical texts and the baptismal covenants. "In the Lutheran Church, we affirm our baptismal covenant to live among God's people, hear God's word, share in the supper, serve all, and strive for justice and peace for all the earth," she said. She talked about the need to keep partisan politics out of advocacy, a reality she

Figure 8.2 Clergy affiliated with Earth Ministry and Washington Interfaith Power & Light gathered at a rally during an EPA hearing in Seattle. Photo by Earth Ministry.

has learned in her eighteen years as a pastor in a church with both Republican and Democratic members. "I consider myself a biblical preacher," she said. "To me, the texts call us to this work. When your activism is rooted in a theological understanding, who can argue with you?"

Pastor Carol had some advice for congregations wanting to bring the environment into the life of their church. Find out what people are already interested in, she recommended. People want to bring their passions to their church life, and clergy have to help them find those places. To that end, the congregation at St. John United has installed low-flow toilets, changed incandescent bulbs to CFLs, added rain barrels to collect water for irrigation, installed a worm bin to vermicompost the soup kitchen's food waste, and composted yard waste.

The church's property committee included several older men who initially challenged the environmental focus of the church, Pastor Carol said. But when the members saw the cost savings of the greening initiatives, they got on board. To date, St. John United has cut its electricity bills by one-third. Much of the funding for the improvements has come from the merger of two churches and the sale of one of the buildings. This church is bringing seeds, sand, and soil into the sanctuary, feeding the hungry from a community garden, affecting policy, and keeping baptismal vows with grace and action. The ministry of bearing witness at St. John United Lutheran Church has not only transformed the church but also made it relevant and viable in this community.

Bearing Witness as a Ministry: Lessons Learned

Christians like LeeAnne Beres, Jessie Dye, Rev. Rich Lang, and Pastor Carol Jensen have articulated the connection between their own faith and action for God's earth in the political arena. Their work reveals key lessons and best practices for other churches wishing to use a prophetic voice in the political process.

Bring together diverse denominations to mobilize the power of the religious voice in the political process.

People of faith have a powerful voice when we organize and advocate in the political arena. Concern about the environment crosses political parties and has the power to bring together diverse constituencies to advocate for specific environmental legislation and action. Across denominations, churches share a moral mandate to care for the earth and steward God's creation. Working together with diverse faith traditions in support of policies and practices can have a greater impact than denominations working alone. Finding common ground around the care of creation is one of the most straightforward ways to ecumenical and interfaith collaboration.

Strategize ways to partner with both faith and secular environmental groups in advocacy for specific pieces of legislation.

In most communities, environmental organizations are working for legislation that promotes healthy environments and connects to Christian values. Partnerships with people of faith present a win-win collaboration. Environmental organizations benefit from the infrastructure and common values of religious groups. Aligning values between these groups can leverage political will and impact.

Clarify the values that connect faith to the care of creation and create spaces for church members to get involved in advocacy.

Why should people of faith care for creation? In Earth Ministry's work, the values include sustainability, stewardship, justice, and spirituality. Members of faith communities can articulate these values in concise ways that show the connection between faith and the environment. Consider organizing a basic training in your church on advocacy skills from a faith perspective. Keep it simple and remember the analogy that advocacy is as easy as ordering pizza. Research the websites of organizations such as Earth Ministry and

Interfaith Power & Light for resources to help organize such training workshops.

> *Take steps toward advocacy by greening a congregation in dimensions such as mission statements, worship, education, institutional life, community outreach, and broader religious outreach.*

Sometimes, churches can approach advocacy through a specific piece of legislation, but taking concurrent steps toward greening a congregation can integrate an inward and outward focus on the environment. Earth Ministry's *Greening Congregations Handbook* should be in every church office, as the book includes concrete steps for greening across a variety of dimensions of church life.

On Reflection

My research in Seattle prompted a strong desire to reclaim my Christianity, as I watched fellow Christians and environmentalists using their faith for advocacy and stewardship. I remember when I began a small wall of icons in my 900-square-foot house after inheriting three icons from my grandfather's collection. After hanging the icons in my living room, I wondered what my Jewish friends might think of my display. I asked my Episcopal priest, "Do you think it looks too Christian?" With an endearing look, as if he were addressing a toddler who had forgotten her name, he said, "Mallory, you are a Christian." With this trip, I grew more comfortable introducing myself by both my vocation and my denomination. The latter label is taking up more space in my self-identity, as I claim my Christian identity in the space of my environmental vocation.

When I was growing up, the emphasis in church seemed to be on being with God in heaven. When someone died, we said, "They are with God in heaven." Rev. Domke's insistence that the kingdom of heaven is *now* stayed with me long after I left Seattle. If the kingdom of God is now, we won't face fancy gates after our deaths, but work awaits us now. I realize today that bearing witness and advocacy are steps toward achieving Jesus' vision of a just and loving world. When we advocate in the name of our faith, we promote a world of peace and equity that includes stewardship of God's resources. From this perspective, advocacy becomes prayer in action.

The words of Rev. Lang also resonated with me, as he modeled liturgy as a radical act. "We are constantly practicing who we are in symbolic form in our liturgy, and then we practice in the world," he said. "We are being trained through the liturgy to live in the world." We repeat the same words each week, so we have a chance of hearing them and enacting them in the world when we leave the sanctuary. Church is like a dress rehearsal for the real deal. My conversations with Rev. Lang, while we ate raspberries and blackberries, awakened me to that baptismal calling of the responsibility we have as children of God: we are called to love and serve our neighbor in the broadest sense, and those duties include caring for creation.

My thoughts of baptism tend toward baptismal gowns, brunches, godparents, and family. I keep a photo in my bedside drawer of my grandfather, the Reverend Cecil Jones, holding me as an infant on my baptism day, after he made the sign of the cross on my forehead and sealed me as Christ's own forever. In the photo, I am held in front of All Saints' Episcopal Church, a tiny wooden church in Mississippi, where I became part of the family of God, with two sets of grandparents by my side, along with aunts and uncles.

My mom once told me that she and my dad couldn't afford nice white baby shoes for my baptism, so she had hidden my feet underneath my baptismal gown for the pictures. By the time her third child came along, my brother's bare feet were hanging out of the gown for all to see. At that time, she could afford the shoes but couldn't imagine spending $20 on shoes for an infant. To me, God is in that story, mirrored in desires that change with age. But I realize that baptism means more than coming into the family of God, but also accepting responsibility to advocate and care for God's creatures in a public arena. We are not only receiving an invitation into the household of Christ. We have to do some domestic chores in the here and now to advocate for creation. And, perhaps, putting our bare feet on the ground, without fancy shoes, is the best place to start.

Conclusion

Acts of Faith Transformed by Grace

The Reverend Kennedy McGowan at First Presbyterian Church in Hollywood, Florida, called it a "God thing." He used this phrase to describe his congregation's work with the Coalition of Immokalee Workers in the Burger King boycott. At some point, the work gained a momentum greater than any individual efforts, resulting in agreements from fast-food companies to increase wages for farmworkers.

Stan Hubbard, the president of Kanuga Conferences, talked about greening as "discernment," a process of listening to the Holy Spirit as a guide and staying open to opportunities. While he searched for ways to finance a solar project, Stan said God led him to pursue a meeting with FLS Energy. Ultimately, this solar company created the financial arrangement that enabled Kanuga to install one of the largest solar hot-water systems in the Southeast.

In her book *Loaves and Fishes*, Dorothy Day speaks of this power—this God thing—that is present in so many of the stories collected for this book. She writes that young people may question the impact of small efforts. "They cannot see that we must lay one brick at a time, take one step at a time; we can be responsible only for the one action of the present moment. But we can beg for an increase of love in our hearts that will vitalize and transform all our individual actions, and know that God will take them and multiply them, as Jesus multiplied the loaves and fishes."[1]

The saints described in this book led ordinary lives touched by both passion and grace: LeeAnne Beres of Earth Ministry, who became a Christian because of the power of the prophetic voice in environmental advocacy; Bishop Charles Jenkins in New Orleans, whose goal was to build affordable, green housing in the Central City neighborhood; Brigitte Gynther with Interfaith Action in South Florida, who worked with congregations as allies in the Campaign for Fair Food; and Katy Hinman, a bat biologist with a master's in divinity who provided a religious response to global warming through Georgia Interfaith Power & Light.

All these natural saints worked for God's good earth by connecting people with places; they were grounded—literally—in a place. Their work mattered to both spiritual and ecological communities, and they continued this work even in the face of seemingly insurmountable challenges, such as corporate spying or large-scale industrial pollution. The people I met in places as diverse as the tomato fields of South Florida and the urban streets of downtown Newark often emphasized the same lessons for the religious environmental movement. Some of those repeated themes were to emphasize the hope that comes from a perspective of faith; integrate prayer and ritual into the environmental movement; create partnerships with other groups doing environmental work; focus on justice; bear witness to the power of stories; and integrate creation into worship, outreach, and education.

As a witness to these stories and strategies, I began to identify these lessons in my own life. One poignant lesson embodies the power of hope, intention, and individual acts that can transform our connection with God and the earth. Two years before my father's unexpected and sudden death, he outlined on a single sheet of paper his plans for what some would call an environmentally sustainable burial. He did not use the words "green" or "environment," but he communicated his wishes for a funeral that relied on family and friends, and not a funeral home. As his grown children, we later followed his wishes, wrapping his body in white linen tablecloths, asking his close friend to build a pine casket, using a pickup truck to transport the casket to the church and the grave site, shoveling dirt on top of the grave, and singing gospel tunes like "I'll Fly Away" with his bluegrass band playing along.

One definition of a saint is someone whose story God is telling.[2] The stories God revealed during this research showed me that my father performed a radical religious act by planning his own home-grown funeral. The God thing has the power to convert our individual, radical acts of faith into a collective force, which is necessary to confront the environmental degradation we face. Our hopeful acts are bold and diverse: one funeral planned, one loaf of communion bread baked, one church garden tilled, one solar panel installed, one cob oven built. Together, we represent a communion of saints, deeply rooted in God's good earth but moving forward, one step at a time.

Afterword

Rev. Brian Cole

"Could you speak with my son?"

The mother and her children are active and faithful members in the cathedral parish where I serve. I knew her son to be a good baseball player, dutiful acolyte, and all-around great kid. Before I told her that I would be willing to speak to him, I began to anticipate what conversation she wanted me to have with him. Could I explain the Trinity? What do Buddhists believe?

"With the long drought we have been having and all these warm winter days, he's worried about global warming. Do you think you could talk to him about his fears?" Okay, not the question I was expecting. When the eleven-year-olds are not sleeping at night because of global warming, then we have entered a new world.

In asking me to speak to her son, the mother hoped I could speak to him about *hope.* Many of the pastoral conversations I have with church members involve hope. Conversations about a new cancer diagnosis, the pain of divorce, a job loss are all opportunities for me to listen and learn with others about how Christians live as hopeful people in the midst of difficult, life-negating times.

At some level, most of those encounters allow me to say something to the effect of, "It's going to be okay." If those words are said too quickly, they come off as patronizing and naïve. Did you really hear me? But if the words are never offered, then what good is faith when life gets broken?

So, how do we speak of hope in the face of climate change? Reading through Dr. McDuff's book, I was reminded of a quote from Thomas Merton, a Catholic monk and mystic who wrote widely across matters both spiritual and political throughout the 1950s and 1960s. In the prologue to his book *Raids on the Unspeakable*, Merton said this: "Christian hope begins where every other hope stands frozen stiff before the face of the Unspeakable."[1]

Merton wrote of the "Unspeakable" as the void, as the "emptiness of 'the end.'" When we reach such a place, true hope is still able to move, to respond, while wishful thinking and naïve assumptions are shown to be hollow and misguided. Hope, true hope, not only does not wither, but actually only begins to be when the crisis becomes evident.

Like the eleven-year-old boy in my parish, many people live in fear of this time; we worry about our deeply distressed planet, with signs of climate change more and more evident. Newspapers and other media often use the word "apocalypse" when they speak of our time. You can hear the ominous organ in the background as they repeat the word: apocalypse . . . apocalypse . . . apocalypse.

However, they do not know what they are saying. The word "apocalypse" originally comes from Greek and means "an unveiling; a lifting of the veil." To live in the time of the apocalypse is not to be situated at *the end* as much as it is to live in a time when things are made plain, when the true measure of things is now known. In other words, in an apocalyptic moment, we learn what kind of people we are. We learn what kind of hope we hold.

By taking us to diverse communities and introducing us to so many faithful Christians who are responding in a variety of ways to our environmental age, Dr. McDuff has shown us what hope looks like now. The environmental crisis is real, and no number of warm vignettes of faithful people allows us to overcome that fact by the next commercial break.

But what is just as real as environmental degradation is the endurance of Christian hope, the willingness to respond in moments when our actions or our work might not make a difference. In those moments, we act because we choose not to be afraid of the unspeakable but instead to be led by the word, the wisdom of God, the Christ.

We do not know what good our work in response to climate change will do for us or for the planet. But we do know that such work will allow the church to continue to be led by the word, the Christ, and not be paralyzed by the fear of the unspeakable.

Such work on behalf of God's creation should be done not because of a naïve and sentimental feeling. I find this sort of sentimental and sweet religious yearning most often expressed by the Christian bric-a-brac images of the thirteenth chapter of First Corinthians, the "love" chapter. The words of St. Paul about love are represented in precious, out-of-context posters and refrigerator magnets. The words of the chapter are actually quite powerful and mature, but they have been domesticated into harmless puffery about love.

At the end of 1 Corinthians 13, however, is a powerful statement against naïve and toothless hoping and wishing. "For now we see in a mirror, dimly, but then we will see face to face. Now I know only in part; then I will know fully, even as I have been fully known. And now faith, hope, and love abide, these three; and the greatest of these is love" (NRSV).

St. Paul reminds us that we live in front of a future that is always a dim mirror. We can deny the not-knowing and rush to assure ourselves that all will be well and good in the future. We can live in fear of the not-knowing and assume the worst, always the worst. Or, we can do what the many natural saints whom Dr. McDuff has met during her travels have done.

They have chosen to live close to the dim mirror, not fearing it or denying it. Actually, it may be possible to love the dim mirror, to trust that what we continue to learn about ourselves in this present moment, with the work God has given us to do now, will go a long way toward shaping the kind of people we will become, the kind of communities in which we live, both now and in the future—whether or not we can control what kind of climate we meet in the future. Hope, however, will keep us moving, not fearing the unspeakable.

St. Paul tells us that both hope and faith are lesser things than love. Faith is the story that finds us in God and forms us in the way of God. Hope is the ability to move when the unspeakable is present.

Love, however, is the strongest force, the force that compels us to respond to God's love, to the love we are given for each other, both stranger and kin, and for the love of God's good creation, which needs to know again that we love it as God has loved it and made it well. This is the moment that is being unveiled.

Notes

Introduction

1. Barbara Brown Taylor, *Leaving Church: A Memoir of Faith* (San Francisco, CA: HarperSanFrancisco, 2006), 227.

2. Richard Louv, *Last Child in the Woods: Saving Our Children from Nature-Deficit Disorder* (Chapel Hill, NC: Algonquin, 2008).

3. Mary Evelyn Tucker, *Worldly Wonder: Religions Enter Their Ecological Phase* (Chicago, IL: Open Court, 2003), 7.

4. J. C. Green, "The American Religious Landscape and Political Attitudes: A Baseline for 2004," *Pew Forum on Religion and Public Life*, http://pewforum.org/publications/surveys/green-full.pdf (accessed Sept. 25, 2009).

5. Lyndsay Moseley and Anna Jane Joyner, *Faith in Action: Communities of Faith Bring Hope for the Planet* (San Francisco, CA: Sierra Club Books, 2008). Also see Lyndsay Moseley, ed., *Holy Ground: A Gathering of Voices on Caring for Creation* (San Francisco, CA: Sierra Club Books, 2008).

6. E. O. Wilson, *Creation: An Appeal to Save Life on Earth* (New York: Norton, 2006), 3, 5.

7. Harper Bibles, *The Green Bible* (San Francisco, CA: HarperOne, 2008).

8. Roger S. Gottlieb, *A Greener Faith: Religious Environmentalism and Our Planet's Future* (New York: Oxford University Press, 2006).

9. Cassandra Carmichael, Laurel Kearns, and Rebecca Gould, "Examining Congregational Components That Lead to Environmental Action," unpublished study, 2007. (For information, contact Cassandra Carmichael,

National Council of Churches Eco-Justice Program, http://www.nccecojustice.org.)

10. Kenneth Woodward, *Making Saints: How the Catholic Church Determines Who Becomes a Saint, Who Doesn't, and Why* (New York: Touchstone, 1996), 13.

Chapter 1

1. Cited in an unpublished handout entitled "Excerpts from Religious Leaders on the Coalition of Immokalee Workers' Campaign for Fair Food" created by Interfaith Action (www.interfaithaction.org). Livingston commented on the agreement between the CIW and McDonald's in his capacity as the president of the National Council of Churches. He now serves as the executive director of the International Council of Community Churches.

2. For a description of twenty-first-century slavery cases in Immokalee, see Presbyterian Church (USA), "Two Sentenced for Slavery: PC (U.S.A.) Calls on Gov. Crist to Act," Dec. 2008, www.pcusa.org/fairfood/2-sentenced-for-slavery.htm (accessed Feb. 6, 2009); and Amy B. Williams, "Immokalee Family Sentenced for Slavery: Each Navarrete Boss Gets 12 Years in Prison," *Fort Myers News-Press*, Dec. 12, 2008, www.sanders.senate.gov/news/record.cfm?id=306164 (accessed June 3, 2009).

3. Noelle Damico, "Accompanying the Coalition of Immokalee Workers during their Fast for Fair Food and Justice, Irvine, California," Feb. 22–Mar. 5, 2003, in the journal of the Reverend Noelle Damico, national coordinator of the Presbyterian Church (USA)'s Fair Food Campaign. Unpublished document. (For more information, contact Noelle Damico, PC (USA) Fair Food Campaign, http://www.pcusa.org/fairfood.)

4. United Methodist Church, "Globalization and Its Impact on Human Dignity and Human Rights," Nov. 25, 1981, http://archives.umc.org/interior.asp?ptid=4&mid=1016 (accessed Feb. 19, 2009).

5. For a discussion of the relationships among the church, human rights, and human dignity, see David Pfrimmer, "A Faith Basis for 60 Years of Human Rights Work by Churches: Evangelical Lutheran Church in America," Feb. 2009, http://www.elca.org/What-We-Believe/Social-Issues/Journal-of-Lutheran-Ethics/Issues/February-2009/3-A-Faith-Basis-for-60-Years.aspx (accessed Feb. 19, 2009); Richard Amesbury and George Newlands, *Faith and Human Rights: Christianity and the Global Struggle for Human Dignity* (Minneapolis, MN: Fortress, 2008).

6. For an overview of wages and poverty levels of agricultural workers in Immokalee, see Coalition of Immokalee Workers, "Facts and Figures on Florida Farmworkers," Apr. 2009, www.ciw-online.org (accessed June 3, 2009).

7. For a descriptive and detailed overview of Immokalee and modern-day slavery in the South Florida fields, see John Bowe, "Nobodies: Does Slavery Exist in America?" *New Yorker*, Apr. 21, 2003.

8. Eric Schlosser details this incident of corporate spying by Burger King on the Student/Farmworker Alliance and the CIW in his editorial "Burger with a Side of Spies," *New York Times*, May 2, 2008.

9. For an overview of the Coalition of Immokalee Workers, see CIW, "About CIW: Consciousness + Commitment = Change: How and Why We Are Organizing," www.ciw-online.org/about.html (accessed June 4, 2009).

10. Leonard Doyle, "Slave Labour That Shames America," *Independent*, Dec. 19, 2007, www.independent.co.uk/news/world/americas/slave-labour-that-shames-america-765881.html (accessed Jan. 15, 2009).

11. Oxfam America, *Like Machines in the Fields: Workers without Rights in U.S. Agriculture* (Boston: Oxfam America, 2003). For an explanation of the negative impacts of fast-food contracts from the growers' perspective, see Charles Porter, "Big Fast-Food Contracts Breaking Tomato Repackers," *Packer*, May 16, 2005.

12. The website of the National Farm Worker Ministry includes a worship service focused on the beatitudes with suggested sermon themes and readings. The site also includes scripture readings related to labor, relevant quotes from leaders such as Cesar Chavez, and a format for a contemplative day on food and labor. See www.nfwm.org/worshipresources/wrshpservice.shtml (accessed June 4, 2009).

13. For a history of the CIW, I used an unpublished document by the Coalition of Immokalee Workers, "¡Golpear a Uno es Golpear a Todos! To Beat One of Us Is to Beat Us All! The Coalition of Immokalee Workers and the Human Rights Framework." Also see Cynthia Soohoo, Catherine Albisa, and Martha Davis, "The Coalition of Immokalee Workers: ¡Golpear a Uno es Golpear a Todos! To Beat One of Us Is to Beat Us All!" in *Bringing Human Rights Home*, vol. 3 (Santa Barbara, CA: Praeger, 2008).

14. See Paulo Freire's *Pedagogy of the Oppressed* (New York: Continuum, 2000).

15. Leonardo Boff and Clodovis Boff, *Introducing Liberation Theology* (Maryknoll, NY: Orbis, 1987).

16. Coalition of Immokalee Workers, "¡Golpear a Uno es Golpear a Todos! To Beat One of Us Is to Beat Us All! The Coalition of Immokalee Workers and the Human Rights Framework." Unpublished document.

17. For an overview of Burger King's decision, see Andrew Martin, "Burger King Grants Raise to Pickers," *New York Times*, May 24, 2008, www.nytimes.com/2008/05/24/business/24farm.html (accessed Jan. 15, 2009).

18. For more information on the Just Faith program, contact Just Faith Ministries, P.O. Box 221348, Louisville, KY 40252, http://www.justfaith.org.

19. Gerardo Reyes-Chavez, "A Letter of Thanks from the Coalition of Immokalee Workers," http://www.pcusa.org/fairfood (accessed Feb. 2, 2009).

20. American Public Health Association, "Toward a Healthy, Sustainable Food System," policy statement, Nov. 6, 2002, http://www.apha.org/advocacy/policy/policysearch/default.htm?id=1361 (accessed June 4, 2009).

21. Gradye Parsons, "Stated Clerk Commends Farmworkers and Whole Foods Market on Landmark Agreement," Sept. 9, 2008, http://www.pcusa.org/pcnews/2008/08655 (accessed Sept. 21, 2009).

22. Mike Hughlett, "McDonald's Farmworker Raise Fought by Growers," *Chicago Tribune*, Nov. 6, 2007, http://archives.chicagotribune.com/2007/nov/06/business/chi-tue_mcd_1106nov06 (accessed June 3, 2009); Elaine Walker, "Subway to Pay More for Tomatoes: An Activist Group Gets Another Fast-Food Chain to Pay More for Tomatoes, but There's Still No Answer on How to Get Money to Workers," *Miami Herald*, Dec. 2, 2008, http://www.miamiherald.com/business/story/796667.html (accessed Jan. 15, 2009).

Chapter 2

1. Elliott Wright, "Faith and Food: Biblical Perspectives," 2001, http://gbgm-umc.org/now/01so/faithnfood.html (accessed Jan. 22, 2009).

2. "On Faith and Food," *Mennonite Brethren Herald*, Sept. 7, 2005, http://www.mbherald.com/44/12/books-2.en.html (accessed Jan. 22, 2009).

3. Sara Miles, *Take This Bread* (New York: Ballantine, 2007).

4. Wright, "Faith and Food: Biblical Perspectives."

5. Holly Lebowitz Rossi, "God in the Garden," *Search Magazine: Science + Religion + Culture*, July–Aug. 2008, http://www.searchmagazine.org/Archives/Back%20Issues/July-August/full-garden.html (accessed Jan. 22, 2009).

6. Wendell Berry, "The Pleasures of Eating," in *Food and Faith: Justice, Joy, and Daily Bread*, ed. Michael Schut (Denver, CO: Morehouse Group, 2002), 142–147. This collection of essays about food and faith addresses a

range of issues, including spirituality and food, hunger and the family farm. Published in collaboration with Earth Ministry, the book includes a study guide for groups and individuals and works well for a discussion group centered on food and faith.

7. Jacob Dagger, "Faith through Food," *Duke Magazine* 94, no. 3. (May–June 2008), http://www.dukemagazine.duke.edu/dukemag/issues/050608/depqa.html (accessed Jan. 22, 2009). This article presents an interview with Duke Divinity School professor Ellen Davis, author of *Scripture, Culture, and Agriculture: An Agrarian Reading of the Bible* (New York: Cambridge University Press, 2008).

8. Rossi, "God in the Garden."

9. Committee on Worship, "A Contemporary Expression of Christian Faith," in *The United Church of Canada Service Book* (Toronto: United Church Publishing House, 1969), 310.

10. National Council of Churches, Eco-Justice Program, "Fresh Food for All," June 26, 2008, http://ecojustice.wordpress.com/2008/06/26/greatgreen-congregations (accessed June 24, 2009).

11. David Dragseth, Margaret Schoewe, and Steve Jerbi, "Congregational Creation Care Stories," *Lutheran Partners: A Bi-Monthly Magazine of the ELCA for Ordained and Lay Leaders* 25, no. 1 (Jan.–Feb. 2009), http://archive.elca.org/lutheranpartners/archives/090102_04.html (accessed June 24, 2009); National Religious Partnership for the Environment, "Fresh Food for All," *NRPE Mainline Protestant Profiles*, http://www.nrpe.org/profiles/profiles_vi_C_33_01.htm (accessed June 24, 2009); National Council of Churches, "Fresh Food for All."

12. Sarah McFarland Taylor, *Green Sisters: A Spiritual Ecology* (Cambridge, MA: Harvard University Press, 2007).

13. Rossi, "God in the Garden."

14. Earth Ministry, *Caring for All Creation: At the Table* (Seattle, WA: Earth Ministry, 2007). This resource kit includes bulletin inserts, flyers, worship services, commitment cards, and educational resources centered on food and faith.

15. "On Faith and Food," *Mennonite Brethren Herald.*

16. David Rosmann and Heather Schoonover, *Faith and Food: Action Strategies for Healthy Eating* (Minneapolis, MN: Institute for Agriculture and Trade Policy, 2009).

17. Michael Schut, ed., *Simpler Living, Compassionate Life: A Christian Perspective* (Denver, CO: Morehouse Group, 2004).

18. Elizabeth Gilbert, *Eat, Pray, Love* (New York: Penguin, 2006).

Chapter 3

1. Note that Carlos's name was changed to protect his identity.

2. Lorna Day, "Designing Sacred Spaces: Sacred Space Can Elevate Our Understanding of Each Other and the World We Share," *United Church Observer*, June 2008, http://www.ucobserver.org/faith/2008/06/sacred_spaces (accessed Mar. 18, 2009).

3. Peter Sawtell, "Will They Hate You?" *Eco-Justice Notes*, Feb. 1, 2008, http://www.nyipl.org/building/green_building.html (accessed Mar. 18, 2009).

4. David Dragseth, Margaret Schoewe, and Steve Jerbi, "Congregational Creation Care Stories," *Lutheran Partners* 25, no. 1 (Jan.–Feb. 2009), http://archive.elca.org/lutheranpartners/archives/090102_04.html (accessed July 9, 2009).

5. Interfaith Power & Light provides this online tool for a congregation to calculate its carbon footprint, as a strategy to identify areas of focus for reducing that footprint. The carbon footprint is divided into four categories: energy use, transportation, goods and services, and waste. For more information, see Regeneration Project and Interfaith Power & Light, "Cool Congregations Calculator," http://www.coolcongregations.com (accessed July 9, 2009). For an overview of the development of the Cool Congregations program, see Lyndsay Moseley and Anna Jane Joyner, *Faith in Action: Communities of Faith Bring Hope for the Planet* (San Francisco, CA: Sierra Club Books, 2008), 13.

6. For an overview of green jobs initiatives in the United States, see http://www.greenforall.org. Green for All is an organization started by Van Jones that promotes green-collar jobs through policy, legislation, programming, and education.

7. For media coverage of the green addition at Pullen Memorial Baptist Church, see Bob Allen, "North Carolina Church Sets Example with Eco-Friendly New Building," *Associated Baptist Press*, Feb. 23, 2009, http://02c22d7. netsolhost.com/PullenDocs/abp_Feb23.html (accessed Mar. 9, 2009); Yonat Shimron, "Raleigh Church Embraces Environmentalism: Church Addition Reflects Congregation's Wish to Help People—and the Earth," *Raleigh News and Observer*, Feb. 2, 2009, http://newsobserver.com/674/story/1390441.html (accessed Mar. 9, 2009).

8. Allen, "North Carolina Church Sets Example with Eco-Friendly New Building."

9. One aspect of this testimony is the fact sheets posted on the church website that explain the details of each of the green features of the addition. The fact sheets cover the general project background and overview, community outreach

for and mission of the expansion, fundraising and financial considerations, caring for youth and children, use of natural daylight, geothermal heating and cooling, and water conservation and storm water management. The fact sheets are available at http://02c22d7.netsolhost.com/PullenDocs (accessed July 9, 2009).

10.   For more information on the Regeneration Project and Interfaith Power & Light, see Suzie Boss, "Praise the Lord, but Dim the Lights: The Regeneration Project Helps the Environmental Movement Get Religion," *Stanford Social Innovation Review* (Spring 2008), 67–68; *The Regeneration Project [and] Interfaith Power & Light Campaign: 2008 Annual Report*, San Francisco, CA.

11.   For video clips and other resources on the religious response to global warming, see http://www.theregenerationproject.org (accessed Sept. 21, 2009).

12.   Sally G. Bingham, *Love God, Heal Earth: 21 Leading Religious Voices Speak Out about Our Sacred Duty to Protect the Environment* (Pittsburgh, PA: St. Lyon's, 2009).

13.   Boss, "Praise the Lord, but Dim the Lights."

14.   GreenFaith, "Building in Good Faith," http://www.buildingingoodfaith.org (accessed July 7, 2009). Also see National Council of Churches, Eco-Justice Program, "Building a Firm Foundation: Green Building Toolkit," http://www.nccecojustice.org/resources.htm/#greenbuildingresources (accessed July 11, 2009).

15.   For one resource on energy efficiency for churches, see National Council of Churches, Eco-Justice Program, "Bottom Line Ministries That Matter: Congregational Stewardship with Energy Efficiency and Clean Energy Technologies," http://www.nccecojustice.org/resources.htm/#greenbuildingresources (accessed July 11, 2009).

16.   GreenFaith, "Building in Good Faith."

17.   North Carolina Interfaith Power & Light, "Project Energize Fact Sheet for Congregations" (Asheville, NC:NC IPL, 2009). Available at: http://www.ncipl.org (accessed March 1, 2010).

Chapter 4

1.   For a discussion of Hurricane Katrina, the future of New Orleans, and a rationale for restoring this city, see Tom Piazza, *Why New Orleans Matters* (New York: Regan, 2005).

2.   Bruce Nolan, "First + Grace = Unity," *Times-Picayune*, Feb. 17, 2008, http://www.nola.com/news/t-p/frontpage/index.ssf?/base/news-10/120322986667440.xml$coll=1 (accessed June 8, 2009).

3. Bruce Nolan, "Louisiana Methodists Have Faith in Post-Katrina Reinvention," *Times-Picayune*, June 6, 2009, http://www.nola.com/news/index. ssf/2009/06/louisiana_methodists_have_fait.html (accessed June 8, 2009).

4. The National Council of Churches is an ecumenical partnership of Christian denominations in the United States, including Protestant, orthodox, evangelical, traditional African American, and living peace churches. The National Council of Churches represents 100,000 congregations and 45 million people. For more information, see http://www.nccusa.org/about/about_ncc.htm (accessed June 11, 2009).

5. Tyler Edgar and Lee Xu, *Climate and Church: How Global Climate Change Will Impact Core Church Ministries* (Washington, DC: National Council of Churches, Eco-Justice Program, 2008).

6. Churches Supporting Churches aims to "restart, reopen, repair, or rebuild" churches to promote congregations as "agents of community development." For details, see http://www.cscneworleans.org/intro.html (accessed June 11, 2009).

7. For a transcript of the Reverend Donald Boutte's testimony, see "Written Testimony by Rev. Donald Boutte to U.S. House of Representatives—Committee on the Budget, Thursday, August 2, 2007, 210 Cannon House Office Building: Hurricanes Katrina and Rita: What Will Be the Long-Term Effect on the Federal Budget," http://budget.house.gov/hearings/2007/08.02boutte_testimony.pdf (accessed June 11, 2009).

8. Leslie Tune, Tronn Moller, Cassandra Carmichael, and Ernest Wright Irving, *Gulf Coast Disaster Response Report: Immediate and Long Term Activities of the National Council of Churches of Christ Member Denominations* (Washington, DC: Special Commission for the Just Rebuilding of the Gulf Coast, National Council of Churches, USA, 2008), 1.

9. Ibid.

10. Episcopal News Service, "Ecumenical Work Week Shows Churches Faithful to Gulf Coast Rebuilding," *Episcopal Life Online*, Aug. 31, 2007, http://www.episcopalchurch.org/79901_89617ENG_HTM (accessed June 25, 2008).

11. Tim Tanton, "Storm Led Churches to 'Dream Big Dreams,' Pastor Says," *Interpreter Magazine*, May 18, 2006, http://www.umc.org/site/c.giJTJbMUluE/b.1693267/k.E514/Storm_led_churches_to_dream_big_dreams_pastor_says.htm (accessed June 25, 2008). This article describes the work of Rev. Cory Sparks at Carrollton and Parker Memorial United Methodist Church. Rev. Sparks currently serves at Faith Community United Methodist Church in Youngsville, Louisiana.

12. Deborah White, "Churches Save Money with Energy Efficient Measures," *Interpreter Magazine*, http://www.umcom.org/site/apps/nlnet/content3.aspx?c=mrLZJ9PFKmG&b=3750135&content_id={74D1B0AF-39BA-4C8E-89F7-B5C23A62E27F}&notoc=1 (accessed June 25, 2008).

13. Ibid. Also see the Green Building Toolkit from the National Council of Churches, available at http://www.nccecojustice.org.

14. For an insider's perspective from the Office of Disaster Response for the Episcopal Bishop of Louisiana, see Courtney Cowart, *An American Awakening: From Ground Zero to Katrina, the People We Are Free to Be* (New York: Seabury, 2008).

15. Bishop Charles Jenkins, "Jericho Road Housing Initiative Is Going Strong," *Bishop's Blog*, Apr. 10, 2008, http://edola-bishop.blogspot.com/2008/04/jericho-road-episcopal-housing.html (accessed June 11, 2009).

16. For a moving account of the impact of Katrina on Bishop Jenkins, see Bruce Nolan, "Episcopal Bishop Charles Jenkins Charts a New Course after Being Traumatized by Hurricane Katrina," *Times-Picayune*, Jan. 17, 2009, http://www.nola.com/news/index.ssf/2009/01/episcopal_bishop_charles_jenki.html(accessed June 11, 2009). This story describes the bishop's spiritual transformation after the hurricane and his decision to leave his position due to symptoms of post-traumatic stress disorder.

Chapter 5

1. GreenFaith, "Health Concerns Related to Diesel Emissions," http://www.greenfaith.org/justice/diesel-factsheet.pdf (accessed June 4, 2009). Also see Clean Air Task Force, "Diesel and Health in America: The Lingering Threat," http://www.catf.us/publications/view/83 (accessed June 4, 2009). To identify exposure to diesel emissions for any zip code in the United States, see Clean Air Task Force, "Diesel," http://www.catf.us/projects/diesel (accessed June 3, 2009).

2. Tom Hayden, *Rebellion in Newark: Official Violence and Ghetto Response* (New York: Vintage, 1967). This book describes the deep roots of environmental injustice in the Newark area.

3. GreenFaith, "Justice: Diesel Emissions in New Jersey," http://www.greenfaith.org/justice/diesel.html (accessed Feb. 2, 2009).

4. Larry Rasmussen, *Earth Community, Earth Ethics* (Maryknoll, NY: Orbis, 1996).

5. For a classic text on environmental justice, see Robert D. Bullard, *Environmental Protection and Communities of Color* (San Francisco, CA: Sierra

Club Books, 1994). For a discussion of the structural racism behind the placement of toxic sites, see Luke W. Cole and Sheila Foster, *From the Ground Up: Environmental Racism and the Rise of the Environmental Justice Movement* (New York: New York University Press, 2001), esp. the section entitled "The Social Structure of Environmental Racism: The Role of Race and Space," 65–70.

6. Many leaders in the environmental justice movement define the environment as "where we live, work, and play." See Patrick Novotny, *Where We Live, Work, and Play: The Environmental Justice Movement and the Struggle for a New Environmentalism* (Westport, CT: Praeger, 2000). Religious environmentalists have added the term "pray" to this definition.

7. Martin V. Melosi, "Environmental Justice, Ecoracism, and Environmental History," in *To Love the Wind and the Rain: African Americans and Environmental History*, ed. Dianne D. Glave and Mark Stoll (Pittsburgh, PA: University of Pittsburgh Press, 2006), 120–132.

8. Commission for Racial Justice, *Toxic Waste and Race in the US: A National Report on the Racial and Socioeconomic Characteristics of Communities with Hazardous Waste Sites* (New York: United Church of Christ, 1987).

9. Mark Stoll, "Religion and African American Environmental Activism," in *To Love the Wind and the Rain: African Americans and Environmental History*, ed. Dianne D. Glave and Mark Stoll (Pittsburgh, PA: University of Pittsburgh Press, 2006), 155.

10. "About GreenFaith," *GreenFaith*, http://www.greenfaith.org/about/index.html (accessed June 5, 2009).

11. Ironbound Community Corporation, "Environmental Justice in the Ironbound, Newark, NJ," unpublished handout provided by the Ironbound Community Corporation and available from GreenFaith (info@GreenFaith.org).

12. "Environmental Justice," *Ironbound Community Corporation*, http://www.ironboundcc.org/node/103 (accessed Sept. 10, 2009).

13. "Our Community," *Ironbound Community Corporation*, http://www.ironboundcc.org/node/109 (accessed Sept. 10, 2009).

14. Cerrell Associates, *Political Difficulties Facing Waste-to-Energy Conversion Plant Siting* (Sacramento, CA: California Waste Management, 1984).

15. "Principles of Environmental Justice," First National People of Color Environmental Justice Summit, Oct. 24–27, 1991, http://www.ejnet.org/ej/principles/html (accessed Sept. 10, 2009).

16. "Integrated Pest Management (IPM) Principles," *Environmental Protection Agency*, http://www.epa.gov/oppo0001/factsheets/ipm/htm (accessed Sept. 10, 2009). This fact sheet describes the basis of IPM as pest management

strategies that do the least amount of harm to both people and the environment.

17. "Religious Principles of Environmental Justice," *GreenFaith*, http://www.greenfaith.org/justice/principles.html (accessed Sept. 11, 2009).

18. Paul Hawken, *Blessed Unrest: How the Largest Movement in the World Came into Being and Why No One Saw It Coming* (New York: Viking, 2007).

Chapter 6

1. Robert Salyer, dir., *Sludge* (Whitesburg, KY: Appalshop, 2005). This documentary film tells the story of the Martin County environmental and health disaster; available at http://appalshop.org/sludge/about/php (accessed Sept. 9, 2009).

2. For more details about Mickey McCoy's activism and the fight against mountaintop removal, see Erik Reece, *Lost Mountain* (New York: Riverhead, 2006).

3. Graham Averill, "The Coal Truth," *Blue Ridge Outdoors* (Mar. 2009), 25–28. (A coal seam is a stratum of coal thick enough for mining.)

4. Ibid.

5. John Eade and Michael Sallnow, eds., *Contesting the Sacred: The Anthropology of Christian Pilgrimage* (Chicago: University of Illinois Press, 2000).

6. For a collection of resolutions by diverse denominations against mountaintop removal, see "Resolutions of Faith," http://www.ilovemountains.org/resolutions (accessed Aug. 19, 2009).

7. Jeff Biggers, "This Little (Coal-Fired) Light of Mine: Will President Heed 45 Million Prayers?" Aug. 2, 2009, http://www.huffingtonpost.com/jeff-biggers/this-little-coal-fired-li_b_249657.html (accessed Aug. 6, 2009).

8. Harry Caudill, *Night Comes to the Cumberlands: A Biography of a Depressed Area*, 2nd ed. (1962; Ashland, KY: Jesse Stuart Foundation, 2001), x.

9. "Frequently Asked Questions about Mountaintop Removal Coal Mining," handout provided by Kentuckians for the Commonwealth during mountaintop removal tour and available at: info@kftc.org.

10. Ibid.

11. Ann Pancake, *Strange as This Weather Has Been* (Berkeley, CA: Counterpoint, 2007); Shirley Stewart Barry, *Bringing Down the Mountains: The Impact of Mountaintop Removal on Southern West Virginia Communities* (Morganton: West Virginia University Press, 2007).

12. J. Matthew Sleeth is the author of *Serve God, Save the Planet: A Christian Call to Action* (White River Junction, VT: Chelsea Green, 2006).

13. Environmental and Public Protection Cabinet, "Citations Issued in Blasting Accident in Hazard," Oct. 21, 2005, http://migration.kentucky.gov/Newsroom/environment/hazardblasting.htm (accessed Aug. 28, 2009).

14. "Frequently Asked Questions about Mountaintop Removal Coal Mining," handout provided by Kentuckians for the Commonwealth.

15. Ilio Delio, Keith Douglas Warner, and Pamela Wood, *Care for Creation: A Franciscan Spirituality of the Earth* (Cincinnati, OH: Saint Anthony Messenger Press, 2009).

16. Ibid.

17. Catholic Committee of Appalachia, *At Home in the Web of Life: A Pastoral Message on Sustainable Communities in Appalachia* (Webster Springs, WV: Catholic Committee of Appalachia, 1995).

18. Wendell Berry, "Speech against the State Government, Frankfort, 2/14/08," www.youtube.com/watch?v=qgfMu2NxtZI (accessed Sept. 25, 2009).

19. Harper Bibles, *The Green Bible* (San Francisco, CA: HarperOne, 2008).

20. Sam Hamilton-Poole, *Earth Gospel: A Guide to Prayer for God's Creation* (Nashville, TN: Upper Room, 2009).

21. "Resolutions of Faith," http://www.ilovemountains.org/resolutions (accessed Aug. 19, 2009).

22. "Peace Advocate Rev. Clinton Marsh Dies at 86," Nov. 4, 2002, http://www.witherspoonsociety.org/clinton_marsh.htm (accessed Aug. 25, 2009). Clinton read this benediction at the end of each General Assembly Peace Breakfast. He was the chairperson of the Presbyterian Peace Fellowship and died on All Saints Day 2002.

23. David A. Kolb, *Experiential Learning: Experience as the Source of Learning and Development* (Upper Saddle River, New Jersey: Prentice-Hall, 1984).

24. Elizabeth Roberts, *Earth Prayers from around the World: 365 Prayers, Poems, and Invocations for Honoring the Earth* (San Francisco, CA: HarperOne, 1991).

Chapter 7

1. Tracy Herzer, *Journey to Adulthood: A Program for Spiritual Formation for Young People* (Leeds, MA: Leader Resources, 2005).

2. Jerome W. Berryman, *Complete Guide to Godly Play*, vol. 1: *How to Lead Godly Play Lessons* (New York: Church Publishing, 2002).

3. Richard Louv, *Last Child in the Woods: Saving Our Children from Nature-Deficit Disorder* (Chapel Hill, NC: Algonquin, 2008).

4. "No Child Left Inside," *No Child Left Inside Coalition*, http://www.cbf.org/page.aspx?pid=687 (accessed Sept. 5, 2009).

5. "About Us: Purpose Statement," *Kanuga*, http://www.kanuga.org/aboutus/purpose.asp (accessed Sept. 5, 2009).

6. Dean Ohlman, "Christian Camps and God's Two Books," *Wonder of Creation*, comment posted Jan. 9, 2009, http://www.wonderofcreation.org/tag/outdoor-education (accessed Aug. 31, 2009).

7. For a history of Kanuga, see Jack Reak, *Kanuga: Story of a Gathering Place* (Hendersonville, NC: Kanuga Conferences, 1993).

8. Dale Neal, "Kanuga Gets Greener with Solar Thermal Hot Water System," Asheville *Citizen-Times*, Jan. 27, 2009, http://www.flsenergy.com/news.php (accessed Aug. 8, 2009). Also see "Kanuga Installs Region's Largest Solar Hot Water System," *Kanuga News* (Spring 2009), 1; Phina Borgeson, "Kanuga Continues Commitment to Sustainability," Episcopal News Service, http://www.flsenergy.com/news.php (accessed Aug. 8, 2009); James Shea, "Kanuga Turns to Solar Power," Hendersonville *Times-News*, Apr. 4, 2009.

9. Ron Mattocks, "Finding Financial Fortitude: How Nonprofits Can Deal with Six Major Threats to Christian Camping," *Christian Camp and Conference Association InSite*, Jan.–Feb. 2009, http://www.ccca.org (accessed Aug. 31, 2009).

10. Teresa Bukner, "Mars Hill College Announces Solar Energy Project," press release, Aug. 13, 2009, Mars Hill College, Mars Hill, North Carolina.

11. Matthew Fox, *Creation Spirituality: Liberating Gifts for the Peoples of the Earth* (San Francisco, CA: HarperOne, 1991), 1.

12. Adapted from Rosemary Radford Ruether, "Creation Spirituality: The Message and the Movement: What Is Creation Spirituality?" *Creation Spirituality Magazine* (Nov.–Dec. 1990),http://www.theoblogical.org/dlature/itseminary/creaspir/whatis1.html (accessed Sept. 5, 2009).

13. "Jubilee! Community Nurture Program," http://www.jubileecommunity.org/nurture.htm (accessed Aug. 31, 2009). Note that, in its publications, Jubilee! uses an exclamation mark in its name. I did not use the punctuation to facilitate ease of reading in the text.

14. Jerome W. Berryman, *Complete Guide to Godly Play*, vol. 1: *How to Lead Godly Play Lessons* (New York: Church Publishing, 2002).

15. Diane Tillman, *Living Values Activities for Young Adults* (Deerfield Beach, FL: HCI, 2001).

16. Starhawk, Diane Baker, and Anne Hill, *Circle Round: Raising Children in the Goddess Traditions* (New York: Bantam, 1998).

17. "The Tree of Contemplative Practices," *Center for Contemplative Mind in Society*, http://www.contemplativemind.org/practices/tree/html (accessed Sept. 5, 2009).

18. For specific ideas for Sunday school initiatives centered on the environment, see "Resources for Youth, Children, and All Ages," *Evangelical Environmental Network and Creation Care Magazine*, http://www.creationcare.org/resources/sunday/youth.php (accessed Aug. 26, 2009). Georgia Interfaith Power & Light also offers a Green Vacation Bible School Curriculum and a middle-school and high-school creation care curriculum. For more information, see http://www.gipl.org/learn.html (accessed Aug. 26, 2009).

Chapter 8

1. "Action: Sign the Call to Care," *Irreplaceable: Wildlife in a Warming World*, 2008, http://www.gao.org/campaign/call_to_care (accessed June 25, 2009).

2. Froma Harrop, "The Unchurched Northwest," *Seattle Times*, Oct. 11, 2005, http://seattletimes.nwsource.com/html/opinion/2002552768_harrop11.html (accessed June 25, 2009). For additional discussion of the interplay of history and religion in this region, see Patricia O'Connell and Mark Silk, eds., *Religion and Public Life in the Pacific Northwest* (Lanham, MD: AltaMira, 2004).

3. Janet Tu, "The Greening of Faith Goes Forth in Seattle," *Seattle Times*, Apr. 14, 2007.

4. LeeAnne Beres, "Grounded in Faith on Our Three-legged Stool," *Earth Letter* (Autumn 2007), 1.

5. For an overview of the Greening Congregations program, see Jessie Dye, "The Eco-Friendly Congregation," *Church and Worship Technology* (Apr. 2008), 46–56. Examples of green congregations are also available on the Earth Ministry website: http://www.earth-ministry.org.

6. "LeeAnne Beres EPA Climate Testimony," *Earth Ministry*, http://www.earthministry.org/resources/success-stories/past-earth-ministry-events/seattle-climate-rally-epa-hearing/leeanne-beres-epa-climate-testimony (accessed June 25, 2009).

7. For examples of staff editorials, see Dan Ritzman and LeeAnne Beres, "Governor Gregoire Must Lead Washington beyond Its Reliance on Coal," *Seattle Times*, Apr. 9, 2009, http://seattletimes.nwsource.com/html/opinion/2009015513_opinc10sierra.html (accessed June 25, 2009); Jessie Dye, "A Morally Acceptable Solution to Climate Change," *Seattle Times*, May 6,

2009, http://seattletimes.nwsource.com/html/opinion/2009185053_opinc07dye.html (accessed June 25, 2009).

8.   "2009 Environmental Priorities," *Environmental Priorities Coalition*, http://www.environmentalpriorities.org (accessed June 25, 2009).

9.   Interfaith Power & Light is an interfaith religious response to global warming with affiliates in 30 states. For more information, see http://theregenerationproject.org; and for the Washington Interfaith Power & Light specifically, see http://earthministry.org/programs/waipl.

10.   Earth Ministry, "Advocacy for All Creation: A Faithful Citizen's Guide to Participating in a Democracy," unpublished document. Available from Earth Ministry (emoffice@earthministry.org).

11.   LeeAnne Beres, "Faith and Advocacy Sermon," First Congregational United Church of Christ, Walla Walla, Washington, Aug. 3, 2008.

12.   Ibid.

13.   Tonya Marcovna Barnett, *Greening Congregations Handbook* (Seattle, WA: Earth Ministry, 2002).

14.   Cassandra Carmichael, Laurel Kearns, and Rebecca Gould, "Examining Congregational Components That Lead to Environmental Action," unpublished study, 2007. (For information, contact Cassandra Carmichael, National Council of Churches Eco-Justice Program http://www.nccecojustice.org.)

15.   The educational modules published by Earth Ministry include the following four-part program: Earth Ministry, *Caring for All Creation: On the Road; At the Table; In the Home; By the Waters* (Seattle, WA: Earth Ministry, 2007). This series addresses the issues of transportation, food, energy efficiency, toxics, and water conservation, all from a biblical perspective, with resources for worship, Sunday school classes, behavior change, and education.

Conclusion

1.   Dorothy Day, *Loaves and Fishes: The Inspiring Story of the Catholic Worker Movement* (Maryknoll, NY: Orbis, 1997), 176.

2.   Kenneth Woodward, *Making Saints: How the Catholic Church Determines Who Becomes a Saint, Who Doesn't, and Why* (New York: Touchstone, 1996).

Afterword

1.   Thomas Merton, *Raids on the Unspeakable* (New York: New Directions, 1966), 6.

Index

Fox, Matthew, 161
Fresh Food for All ministry, 42

Gallup study, 35, 53
gardening, 33, 43–46, 52
Garden Plot to Kitchen Pot, 50
Garland, Sheldon, 117
Garlock, Vicki, 149, 151–52,
    163–64, 165
Genesis 1:31, 57
Genesis 2, 177
Genesis 2:27, 6
Georgia Interfaith Power & Light
    (GIPL), 75, 76, 99, 198
geothermal system, 68
Gibbs, Lois, 113
Gilbert, Elizabeth, 55
global warming, 61, 74, 191
God, 198–99
    and food, 34–35
Godly Play program, 150, 164
Golden Memorial United Methodist
    Church, 124
Grace Lutheran Church
    CIW's demonstration with the
    buckets, 25
grassroots organizations, 29, 119,
    120 (see also specific
    organizations)
Greater Hood AME Church, 115
Green Bible, The, 7, 142, 146
green building, 58, 61, 74, 77, 79,
    80–82, 101
    design decision making process,
    60, 70–72, 79–80
    justice and job promotion,
    63–66
    as a model for other churches,
    66–69, 78–79
    more than an add-on to church,
    69–79

A Greener Faith: Religious
    Environmentalism and Our
    Planet's Future, 7
GreenFaith, 7, 78, 80, 103–110, 113,
    120–121
Green Habit, 50
Greening Congregations Handbook,
    186, 188, 194
Greening Congregations program,
    175, 186–92
green jobs, 63–66, 78
Green Jobs initiative, 175
Green office spaces, 60
Greenpeace, 19
Green Sisters, 48–49
Grover, Steve, 23
Gynther, Brigitte, 18, 198

Harlan, Will, 137, 144
Harlem Congregations for
    Community Improvement
    (HCCI), 115
Harper, Rev. Fletcher, 103, 105,
    107, 108, 110, 112, 117, 118,
    150
HarperOne, 6–7
Hurt, Truman, 138, 140, 141, 148
Healy, Maureen "Mo," 163
Hill, Reverend Bill, 54
Hinman, Katy, 75, 76–77, 99, 198
hope, 8, 99–100, 148, 198, 201–2,
    203
    power of, 85–89, 110–13, 119
Hope Center, 68
Hubbard, Stan, 151, 155, 156, 157,
    158, 169, 197
human dignity, 11, 12, 13, 14
    protecting as a ministry, 28–32
    and sustainable food systems,
    26–28, 30
human rights, 13, 16